LETTERS FROM HASTINGS

PIERRE TEILHARD DE CHARDIN

LETTERS
FROM HASTINGS

1908–1912

INTRODUCTION BY HENRI DE LUBAC, S.J.

HERDER AND HERDER

1968
HERDER AND HERDER NEW YORK
232 Madison Avenue, New York, N.Y. 10016

Original edition: *Lettres d'Hastings et de Paris,*
first half; Paris, Aubier, 1965.
Translated by Judith de Stefano.

LETTERS FROM HASTINGS

INTRODUCTION

BY HENRI DE LUBAC, S.J.

The welcome given Pierre Teilhard de Chardin's *Letters from Egypt* has prompted us to publish the letters which he wrote to his parents with a remarkable regularity from the time he returned from Cairo in the summer of 1908 until he entered the army in December of 1914. At first, we simply thought of including a few extracts rather than every letter. But the public demands to know everything about a great man, and there is a very good cause for such curiosity. Thus, with the consent of the family of Father Teilhard, we have decided to publish the entire text, even though a few of the letters do not tell us very much about their author.

For four consecutive years, from 1908 to 1912, Pierre Teilhard was in Sussex, England, at the scholasticate of Ore Place, near the town of Hastings. Following the normal course of studies to become a Jesuit, he completely devoted himself to theology and was ordained to the priesthood.

Unassuming in his ministry, he became more involved in his scientific studies. He knew his father and brothers were very interested in his work, and therefore his daily routine, news of the family, birthdays, his thoughts about contemporary events, details of his walks and travels occupy a great part of his letters. Picturesque descriptions abound here as they did in his *Letters from Egypt*. Those who know the English countryside of Sussex and Kent will recognize the charm of its hills, valleys, its small villages, its old castles, and large parks. Pierre Teilhard sees it all, both as painter and scholar: it may be a hillside in the spring, a ceremonial procession, a storm at sea, some farmers at a fair, some herons building their nest; forms, colors, and movements are all recorded with precision. One day, a herd of cattle blocked his way: he knew there were sixty-three.

It was during a walk about the outskirts of Hastings in May, 1909, that he met the amateur geologist Charles Dawson. The two found each other good company and became friends. Three years later, on April 26, 1912, a letter mentions the recent visit of Dawson to Ore Place: "He brought me some pre-historic remains (silex, an elephant's tooth, and one from a hippopotamus, and even some fragments of a human skull, which were very thick and well preserved) which he found in some alluvium deposits not far from here, in order to entice me to go out and do the same; but I hardly have any more time for that." Nevertheless, towards the end of May Pierre Teilhard accompanied Dawson for the first time to the area of Piltdown, near Uckfield; they were joined by Professor Woodward, the director of the paleontological division of the British Museum. While Dawson found a new fragment of a human skull, Teilhard found an elephant molar: "This first elephant tooth made me feel like a hunter after his first catch." On August 30, 1913, the three hunters found themselves at the same site on a new expedition. It was on that day that Pierre Teilhard had the "good fortune"—or bad fortune

—to find "the canine tooth from the jaw of the famous Piltdown Man."

His letters from England not only included questions of geology and pre-historical data, but also matters of botany, entomology, and ornithology; theology was not mentioned nearly as much. Not once is any faculty member of Ore Place mentioned by name. There are some allusions to school exercises or preparations for an exam, but none is really sufficient to tell us much about the essential work of Pierre Teilhard. A casual mention about the "death of poor Tyrrell" or the first "delivery of a sermon, ordered by Pius X," does not give us a very clear picture of life in the scholasticate during this time of reaction against modernism. Nor can we tell what were his thoughts about doctrinal matters of his day. But we must not be deceived by the absence of such information. Theology was highly honored at Ore Place and everyone seriously devoted himself to its study . . . a seriousness that would seem superhuman today.

We also learn a little about the spiritual life of this young religious from his letters. The approaching of priesthood, Marguerite-Marie's illness, the death of Françoise in China, various family incidents, all bring it to the fore. As in his previous letters, Pierre, now almost thirty years old, was still affectionate and understanding with his parents; he spoke to them about religion without frills or affectation; some of his advice which would seem pretentious from someone else, coming from Pierre Teilhard expresses a sincere and deep piety that needs no explanation. No theories are proffered, nothing that resembles an outline of the organized doctrine that he will teach in *The Divine Milieu;* but in each circumstance there is a definite reminder of principles that will never cease to guide his own life. "God alone

7

is the End of all things"; . . . "the good life is that which fulfills God's plans"; . . . "His will is the only absolutely necessary and most valued thing on earth; it alone is permanent and takes precedent over all." We must "see the hand of God in every event." All separation, all proof (he will say later: all passivity), must lead to "Him who must grow in us, filling up the vacuum that is left; He alone is capable of achieving this." That is what he will say over and over to his father and mother, as he will say again and again to himself, as he will repeat to everyone.

When, after the experience of the war years, Pierre Teilhard will work out his scientific and apologetic work "in forty years of continued reflection," he will not have to deny, nor even modify, these fundamental truths. All the rest, which he only caught a glimpse of before 1914, will serve, so to speak, as prolegomena. He will continue to establish a firmer foundation for them and bring them into greater clarity. It is in this fidelity to the "Necessarily and Sufficiently Unique" that he will live and die.

1

Amiens, Sunday Evening
[September 1908]

Dear Father and Mother,

I'm taking advantage of a drawn-out wait for the train to tell
you a bit of what has happened since I left.[1] At Vichy, I had no
trouble at all finding the train. Yéyé's directions were good. I
arrived in Paris after a pleasant evening. I only resumed the trip
this morning after having done almost everything I wanted.
Since Father de Joannis[2] was out of town, I didn't get to see him.

1. Returning from a three-year "residence" at the College of the Holy
Family in Cairo (see *Letters from Egypt, 1905–1908* [New York, 1965],
Pierre Teilhard, who is not a priest yet, has just spent a few days with
his family in Auvergne. He is now going to pay a visit to his older sister
Françoise, a Little Sister of the Poor, in Amiens, before going on to the
scholasticate in England to study theology.
2. Father Joseph de Joannis (1854–1932) was an eminent entomologist.
See *Annales de la Société entomologique de France,* vol. 103 (1934), and
Etablissements des Jésuites en France depuis quatre siècles (a work published under the direction of Father Pierre Delattre), vol. 4, art. "Poitiers"
(by Father de La Rochebrochard). (This "Dictionary of Reviews" in five
volumes in-4°, which is often cited, has been edited in Belgium [1940–
1957]; today, a unique storehouse of knowledge: H. Beylard, 35 rue de
Voltaire, Lille, 59).

I did see quite a bit of Robert du Buysson. Friday evening, I had dinner with him and Paul du Ranquet. I would never have believed the lab entomologist from the Museum could be so spiritual and such a fine conversationalist. He spoke about Tunisia, I about Egypt. At the laboratory, he took me around to the collections which Yéyé and Biel know so well. But I will write to them separately about that. In any case, what he knew about my Egyptian "Chrysis" astounded me.

Earlier the same day I had luncheon with my friend Couyat the mineralogist, and another "Egyptian," who had accompanied M. Clermont-Ganneau to the excavations at Aswan. It was a gay time and they smoked real Egyptian cigarettes from Cairo. M. Couyat introduced me to M. Lacroix, the man from Mt. Pelée and Mt. Etna, who was just returning from Murols and Lioran.

Just by chance, I ran into my old friend Bovier-Lapierre,[3] a naturalist and biologist with whom I had seen the famous diplodorus dinosaur.

Finally, yesterday, I went to see Aunt Louise who was just in the middle of making a retreat. To see her, I had to get permission from Mother Néreux. Aunt Louise[4] was the same as ever, very holy and reminding me very much of Mother. Since Mother Néreux was having a conference with Reverend Mother General, I couldn't see her; but I think that with a bit more persuasion, they would have called her for me.

Then this morning, I left for Amiens. More or less unfortunately, I dropped by rue Jules Barni. It was at the end of a

3. See *Letters from Egypt,* letter 4.
4. A member of the religious order of women called Madams of the Sacred Heart. She was the younger sister of Berthe de Dompierre d'Hornoy, the mother of Father Teilhard.

retreat for the old people, and Françoise received me in the kitchen.[5] All the same, we ate together and visited at length. Guiguite is very wrong to think of her as being nailed down by austerity. I gave her all the family news, but she will have to write to you for the rest. I saw some of the old people at the home, especially the old men entrusted to Françoise's care. They are numerous and seem very kind. I also saw Sister Delphine and stayed to chant the office with the community. If Françoise does get a new assistant, it will be during the week, for the one she has is leaving Amiens tomorrow.[6]

The most delicious grapes I've ever tasted, grow all over the convent trellis. It seems that all the old folks there know our family well. After all, in the past year, all of us except Guiguite have been there for a visit. But I don't know whether they really will have understood what my dressing as a clergyman really means.

Now I'm in the snack-bar in Amiens; before coming, I toured the cathedral. Pitch dark out though it was, I wandered by some of the back streets which brought memories from the past 20 years. I vaguely recalled Chantilly as well, and Clermont's pastures. Now I won't see anything until I reach Dover.

Goodbye for now. My love to you, Guiguite, Biel, Yéyé, Joseph, Gonz., and Victor.[7]

5. Françoise was to write her father on September 17th: "I hope life in Cairo has not tired him out too much. He has lost weight but is happy nonetheless. You should be very proud of him. He is kinder than ever before and is still as good and serious as ever."

6. See letter 7.

7. His sister: Marguerite-Marie; his younger brothers: Gabriel, Olivier, Joseph, Gonzague, and Victor. See *Jeunesse et Vocation de Pierre Teilhard de Chardin*, by A. Demoment, in the review *Ecclesia*, no. 162 (Paris, 1962).

When you are ready to leave, there is the temptation to convince yourself that it would be better not to see each other again, but you realize that it's wrong to think like that. After these get-togethers, we love each other more. I'll send you a card from Ore.

Pierre

2

Ore Place, Hastings
September 18, '08

Dear Biel and Yéyé,

After the great time we had together, I thought I'd write to you. I don't suppose that it will be the last letter of the year to one of you or the other. To begin, I'm going to give you some idea of my new impressions of England. First of all, I arrived safely.[1] A fast train took me to the Calais-Maritime dock. The steamer was waiting there, all aglow from the beacons in the light house and from the moon which was still quite radiant. Even though you could see very little, the night crossing was rather pleasant; in any case, it was a short one, and at dawn, the

1. He came to the house at Ore Place, near Hastings (Sussex, England). There, in a rather large, fairly new building overlooking the town, the Jesuits from Lyons and Paris (who emigrated from Lyon-Fourvière to Canterbury in 1901) established their scholasticate in 1906. These Jesuits were to return to Lyon-Fourvière in 1926. (See *Etablissements, op. cit.,* vol. 2, art. "Hastings" by Louis Rosette.)

During his four years of theology, Pierre Teilhard's rector was Father Auguste Bulot.

13

boat was steaming along at a good clip. The sea was extremely gentle, but this didn't keep more than one passenger from getting seasick. Around 3 A.M., I reached Dover. Since the train was to leave only at 6:30, I had the leisure to watch the bevy of trains for London. To be sure, the Exposition and the Congress have attracted a considerable number of spectators, and they probably needed an extra train. Meantime, I had hot chocolate and then found the South-Eastern Railway station without any trouble.

It's a three hour trip from Dover to Hastings with a long stop at Ashford.

As far as Folkestone, the track follows the great white cliffs. After that, it goes through rolling green fields dotted with large grounds and many sheep and starlings. That will be my surroundings for the next four years. You already know what the house looks like; but I've enclosed a new picture with an "x" marked over my room. I might add that things here are generally made of red brick; if I am so influenced by preconceived notions, then I must learn to brush off the unexpected. My room faces west, with a view comparable to Montgascon: mainly wooded land as far as the eye can see, and a portion of the sea. From the turret of the house (at the right in the picture), there's a sweeping view of the sea which is constantly furrowed by the many different boats ranging from colossal transatlantic ships to the common cargo vessels. All of them pass relatively close to the shore. At the same time, we're quite far from the water, about an hour's walk. At the foot of a wooded promontory, between Ore Place and the beach, Hastings spreads out its multitude of small cottages—often clustered and soldered 10 or 20 together, all identical like the rings on a caterpillar. There seem to be some magnificent piers, the "Parade"; and evidently it's a fashionable town, but I haven't seen much of it yet.

You can see dozens of very blond, blue-eyed youngsters; either dreadfully dirty or extremely clean, young boyish-looking girls, workers with small, down-curving moustaches; farmers clean-shaven except for a bristle or two under the chin. Near here is the road to London. It is used by cars, but you can also see Englishmen with capes and pipes, and elderly ladies strolling along it. There are some rather large grounds around the house. They have more or less uncultivated sections overrun by gorse bushes, large hedges, small oaks, meadows and cows. It's very countryish, and so, pleasant and relaxing.

I've found many old friends here, and I'm waiting for the best of them, Father de Bélinay[2] and Father de Jerphanion.[3] They'll arrive at the end of the month.

Classes begin October 5th. It seems that they are packed and don't allow for free time. It's an inconvenience everyone sees but can't remedy.

Naturally one of my first preoccupations was to see what the countryside had to offer. Geologically speaking, this is a lower cretaceous area (approximately 120,000,000 years old) marked by chalky soil, the extinction of dinosaurs, the development of early mammals and flowering plants, and I've already spotted a few fossils. In the cliffs are slender threads of lignite, compressed like jet and containing pretty leaf impressions. I think I'll start collecting insects too. Talking about insects, the only way to classify

2. See *Letters from Egypt,* letter 1.
3. Father Guillaume de Jerphanion (1877–1948) a member of the Institute, archeologist, was the first to explore the rupestral churches in Cappadocia. See *Etablissements, op. cit.,* vol. 4, art. "Villefranche Mongré" by A. Demoment, and *Grand Larousse encyclopédique,* vol. 6.

15

the collections is the one I described to Biel; M. du Buysson divides each box into a certain number of rows with red thread, and fills them one by one going in a line according to each species. It's infinitely clearer that way. Among other things, he had some weevils from Mont Dore—the "avernicus" species (a bit analogous to the bronze, birch variety we have, but browner) which lives in the sorb trees. He also told me about a curious species of fly, the xenos (class: strepsiptera). They are small flies (the females are wingless and the males have two fan-shaped wings) whose parasitic larva live upon the hymenoptera. The larva can be seen easily: it lifts up segments of the abdomen and makes a nest there. When such a hymenoptera is found, try to nourish it in a box with a bit of honey and wait for the xenos to hatch. It's a rare, little-known kind of insect: it doesn't have a mouth and dies quickly. The *polistes* wasp is frequently victimized and is easy to raise.[4]

I saw M. de Genouillac in Paris, but neither Father Desribes[5] nor Father de Joannis who was on vacation.

Goodbye now, to you and Joseph. Our Lord was very good to allow us to see each other again as we did.

Show this letter to Father and Mother. My love to them and to you as well.

Pierre

4. Gabriel and Olivier were themselves deeply interested in the natural sciences; Emmanuel, their father, initiated them from childhood.
5. Pierre Teilhard had Father Desribes as a science professor in Mongré.

3

Dear Father and Mother,

It still surprises me when your answers come so quickly after my letters; that makes it all the more pleasant.

By contrast, I really regret that your vacation has ended, especially this year, judging what I could by the vivid and gay September in Vialles—even though some are missing. I didn't write on the 27th, but you knew very well that I was with you in spirit and remembered him whom we all think about but do not mention often.[1]

The poor Molochs[2] leave tonight. You know that I'm with quite a few of Gonzague's and Victor's teachers and supervisors, Father Lenoir[3] in particular. He mentioned Gonzague to me;

1. The anniversary of Albéric's death, the eldest of the family. See *Letters from Egypt,* letters 11 and 26.
2. Family name of the youngest.
3. Father Louis Lenoir (see *Letters from Egypt,* letter 51), about to begin theology, had just finished his regency at Marneffe, where Gonzague and Victor were students. Regarding this college, opened between Namur

basically, I believe that all of poor Gonzague's troubles stem from his wildness; I doubt that anyone recognized his real worth. Admittedly, he does little to help it along. So, we're coming back Monday and I'm not asking for better; Egypt is hard to forget. Meanwhile, after a healthy amount of rain and fog, England is trying its best to look pretty. For the past few days, the weather has been marvelous, so beautiful in fact, that yesterday, we were allowed to take an all-day trip to the country. It's a pleasant custom to do this almost every month. Thanks to Father de Bélinay's thorough acquaintance with the place, I made a 40 kilometer jaunt with him—a distance sufficient to give me a good idea of the terrain. First, there is a number of well-used, mostly-narrow trails which cross without altering the flow of the land; they multiply the downs, and especially the ups. Even so, they are pleasant to follow because they are frequently in the middle of a park or woods. These parks and woods (often both at the same time) seem to take up about a third of the area, and they are pleasant for the walker. They are always crossed by a few public paths, marked with signs saying "foodpass,"[4] or fences with gates to allow for crossing the enclosures. One of the land-owners, Lord Ashburnham, has given us the freedom to go all through his estate which means that we can walk in wooded land for hours. These woods are varied; most often they're huge saplings mixed in with beautiful old trees. But there are also full-grown forests of beeches, oaks and pines.

Planted at regular intervals among other trees on the grounds

and Liège by the French Jesuits in exile, see *Etablissements, op. cit.*, vol. 3, art. "Marneffe," by M. d'Ambrières.

4. The French text reads "foodpass." This is probably Father Teilhard's phonetic rendering of "footpath." —Tr.

are some beautiful Wellingtonia. There are pheasants all over; they can be seen running in the meadows or flying off at the end of a field. When you come upon houses, they are always extremely clean, with curtains and flower boxes in the windows, little, carefully tended gardens, and ivy covering the front. Some of these vines make magnificent purple covers, and they remind me of Guiguite. Yesterday, for the first time in a while, I felt my feet getting soaked as I crossed the meadows or other damp places. Father will certainly take to the place and he will have the chance to see for himself. Twice during my wanderings, I had the chance to go to Battle where the famous William the Conqueror fought. Beside the small town, there is an extremely pretty and very old abbey, something else you most certainly will go to see when you are here.

Enclosed for Guiguite is a postcard (which Madame Burdo gave me, among others, when she was told that I had admired similar ones at Christian's[5]); this postcard is doubly true-to-life as far as its arrangement of places and the condition of the sky. A small cross in the margin shows the approximate position of Ore Place. In the background is the ancient castle of Hastings, or at least its promontory—then a breakwater—finally, hardly visible all the way at the bottom, to the right of the sunspot, is the cape at Eastbourne (Newhaven is on the other side). To the left of the card, beautiful cliffs stretch out along the coast, where I will have the chance to collect a few fossils.

I just received a letter from Robert du Buysson concerning the Chrysis which I brought to him; you saw it. Besides the Chrysis Zobeida (. . . . .) they know of a male from Aden and another

5. Regarding Father Christian Burdo, see *Letters from Egypt*, letter 32. His widowed mother entered the convent.

is known in (. . . . . .), there's even a Chrysis Teilhardi. It isn't to console me for having left Cairo either.

I was happy about Yéyé's white-necked goose, especially for his sake. I suppose that it will probably be stuffed. I told you that Father de Bélinay is here (for another year yet); he came back from his post in Corrèze. Father de Jerphanion (who is a year ahead of me in theology) hasn't turned up yet; he's on a trip to Paris.

Goodbye, dear parents. My love to you and Guiguite and especially to Joseph; let him try not to be so depressed. My prayers for you.

Pierre

4

Dear Father and Mother,

This letter will arrive in the middle of Joseph's exams and all the anxieties that come with them. I'm waiting for the results with a bit of impatience, and in any case, I wish the candidate heart in the face of whatever fate is set aside for him.

Here, classes began two weeks ago, but the daily schedule won't be followed strictly until tomorrow.[1] Up to now, the work itself hasn't seemed too rough, although there is much more than there was in philosophy. Stress is laid on documentation and textual criticism, which isn't too tiring. As for other things, the fresh air whips up a ferocious appetite and Mother can hope to see me reach the priesthood almost fat. We even have a few sports. Football is played with almost religious fervor (I'm not a regular player yet) to the greatest delight of Englishmen passing by on the road skirting the meadow, stage of our spec-

1. Father Teilhard had these professors during his first year: fundamental theology, Father Frédéric Bouvier; moral theology, Fathers Garde and Rivet; Church history, Father Yves de la Brière.

tacular. You have to be here, for no photo has ever publicized a gang of Jesuits in sweatshirts given over to hearty sports.

With a little astonishment and some pleasure, I noticed that the altar here comes from rue Bensac.[2] That was something I didn't expect to see. However, I have to admit that I only recognized it after someone called my attention to it.

With the exception of a little fog, it's sunny here, something appreciated by the elders in the house. With these conditions, of course, the countryside is very beautiful, and I suppose I shall end up regretting to leave, but it isn't the same as Egypt. During my reading, I discovered that this part of the country (the Weald) is remarkable, geographically speaking; it is made up of secondary deposits from the estuary of a large river and is marked by the remains of giant saurians, iguanodons and others. I've already collected several teeth and fish scales.

From Cairo, we received the sudden and very sad news of Father de Verneuil's death.[3] He was taken away very quickly by a bad case of influenza. It happened just at the start of the new term and the students were deeply moved by it. Personally, I was very grieved.

Goodbye, dear parents. Having seen Sarcenat again allows me to think of you there. It must be very beautiful now. Love and prayers.

Pierre

2. In Clermont-Ferrand, where the Jesuits lived before their expulsion.
3. "Minister" at the College of the Holy Family in Cairo, Father Edouard de Verneuil (1860–1908) was former rector of the Collège de Moulins-Bellevue. "A religious man, who was characteristically kind, prudent and discreet," wrote Father Jean Gautherot in an article entitled "Yzeure," in *Etablissements, op. cit.,* vol. 5.

5

Ore Place, Hastings
November 4, '08

Dear Father and Mother,

I just received Father's letter happily reassuring me that everyone at home is well; I hope that the imposed rest is profitable for those involved, but it's too bad that this snag had to coincide with Central's holiday.[1] At least let those students bring back some woodcocks.

You will find my letter arriving rather late this time; meanwhile, I haven't forgotten you these days, nor especially those who have left us, particularly Loulou whose birthday it would have been.[2] I think we have to remember that all of them are much happier than we could have wished them; and as for ourselves, remember that the sad years will be the best years of our lives in the end, because God inevitably occupied a greater role.

1. Gabriel and Olivier, students at Ecole Central, both finished in 1909. Gabriel specialized in chemical products, Olivier in mining.
2. His little sister, Marie-Louise, died of meningitis. See *Letters from Egypt*, letter 23.

While you were having snow in Auvergne, a sharp cold wave hit here, without a frost, however; and since then, we have had the loveliest weather possible even though it is always very foggy. Tomorrow we have an all-day outing, and I'm going with Father Burdo and Father de Jerphanion to take in the "autumn feast" among the beech trees at Ashburnham. In fact, after the last cold spell, the woodlands not far from here have some magical spots; from my window, I can let myself be charmed by the gilded tops of the birch and beech trees.

A week ago, through a happy error, I strayed into some secluded sections of a large park nearby and found myself in the middle of yellow woods, and large meadows full of cows. Full of joy, and with no fear of meeting up with the constable, we came upon a flock of pheasants in the open, just about nightfall. With a noise like thunder, they were taking off from all corners; a good number had been perched in the beech trees. We finally emerged without any trouble—I forgot to tell you about the number of owls in the country; there are even some near Ore, and from my room, I can hear them singing, which stirs up old and sweet memories of Sarcenat.

I think that eventually I shall find enough to keep me involved in geology; there's hardly a chance of finding something new, but the land is new to me, and can teach me quite a bit. Yesterday, in the crumbling rocks along the shore, I saw a dozen or so iguanodon prints, a classical curiosity in Sussex. This species of saurians used to walk on two bird-like feet, and has left the deep imprints of three large digits, easily 20–30 centimeters long.

One of the priests here went to Marneffe,[3] and I gave him a letter for the Molochs (in regard to this, I still haven't Central's

3. See letter 3, note 3.

address); I made a point of telling them about the memorable fight I saw between a weasel and a fat rat. The outcome? The weasel bled his foe and carried him off.

Goodbye for now. Love and prayers to you and Guiguite.

Pierre

6

Dear Father and Mother,

You will have heard from Central about the happy and unexpected way I visited them last Sunday. Also, they will have
told you why I had to go to Paris: by a fluke, mostly, I was asked
to write an article on Lourdes for *Etudes,* and out of respect for
Mr. Boissarie,[1] who absolutely insisted on telling his story in person, I was sent to see him. Obviously it wasn't disagreeable. Here's
how the trip went. Saturday night at eight, I left for New-Haven,
which is very close to Hastings, and from there, I had a pleasant
crossing to Dieppe. The sea was calm and it only took the
steamer between three and four hours to make the trip. At
Dieppe, there was a train waiting at the dock, and around 7
o'clock, I arrived in Paris. Between Ore Place and Paris, there
was no scenery; and there was hardly anything to see at the end
of the trip, for it was terribly foggy. Biel came to get me at 8

1. Dr. Boissarie was Director of the Bureau of Medical Verifications at
Lourdes.

o'clock; I was able to see him a little in the morning while visiting one of the doctors who had just finished a thesis about Lourdes. I hope to get some information from it. Not knowing the schedule for the day, Yéyé filled out the morning while Biel was digging out information. At 2 in the afternoon, they both came to get me and we chatted as we walked around in the foggy streets near the Eiffel Tower and the Trocadéro. By four o'clock, I found Dr. Boissarie, a fine and friendly fellow, who told me about Lourdes with enthusiasm. He was lucky to find such a beautiful work to which to dedicate his life. I reminded him that Albéric had known his son in Jersey; but I don't know what became of him.

Finally, I arrived at Lion d'Argent around 6 p.m., and Central received me cordially. Yéyé was enjoying Sorel.[2] I was shown some projects, told about the one outlined for the end of the month on scraps of paper, and I looked at a few caricatures of the teachers, etc. Naturally, the story of his cock-hunting escapades found its place. Then we ate at the "Bouillon Duval," a traditional place, so it seems, to bring the family when they go through Paris. They unanimously ordered a kind of beef in memory of Sarcenat.

It was so enjoyable to see those two great men again and we spent a good day. I left Paris on the same train at 9 o'clock and was back in Ore on Monday only having missed one class!

As yet, I haven't mentioned the famous trip to Ashburnham; I wasn't really let down. The park consists of 3 enclosures, more or less concentric, each one taking up almost the same area as Vialles. The outermost is woods (pine or coppice). The second

2. Probably a work not by Georges Sorel but rather by Albert Sorel, *L'Europe et la Révolution française.*

27

encircles some magnificent trees, and borders on large pasture lands where herds of deer and Scottish cattle with thin horns, and long hair, roam. The third, the park itself, accurately speaking, remains just a large woods but has lordly splendor. All the oaks are like the largest ones at Vialles, and the chestnuts are larger than those "of Madame." We came at a time when all these clusters of yellow, gold and red leaves were reflected in the large narrow pools which fill the heart of the small valley. On the outskirts, in the middle of the traditional turf, is a very simple castle that looks as if it could be the one used by the Sleeping Beauty. It is a sad calm, very much in the English mood. Lord Ashburnham is away often; he only has one, very young daughter, and after his death, according to English law, Ashburnham will be turned over to his brothers (who are Protestant). To get there, we had to cross another completely wooded, but much newer park, with rhododendron groves around the castle. There I saw an albino pheasant flying away.

Since then, we have had a cold spell, then a short storm which caused almost all the leaves to fall. But it is still beautiful out even though the days are getting very short.

Goodbye for now. My love and prayers to you and Guiguite.

Pierre

7

Ore Place, Hastings
December 4, '08

Dear Father and Mother,

It's already two weeks since I last wrote. You must be starting to wonder. . . . During this time, I've been quite busy writing my article which is now finished, by the way, but not quite ready for publication; as usual, it has to be revised considerably which means some writing here and there. But at least the bulk of the work is finished.

It upset me to hear of Father's accident at Faumagny. For her feast on December 8, the Blessed Virgin must give all three of you strength. I won't forget to ask Him the same, among other, more important things.

I know that Françoise has cultivated a silence about her work; but I don't think the poor little thing is proud of it at all. While I was there, she was terribly afraid of something hanging over her head.[1]

Here, we are deep in a northern Autumn; it's not very cold,

1. See letter 1.

but it is overcast, misty, or frankly, foggy; one day when the sun condescended to show itself at noon, I was startled to see it so low on the horizon. Under these circumstances, I would prefer to see it lower yet, and I do reproach Ore for not being in Scotland. We have to see everything in its perfection.

Last Monday, an excursion took me to see a lovely corner of Sussex, Winchelsea. If Father were to look on a map, he would find it a bit east of Hastings. It's one of the old Norman cities which, along with Hastings, Rye and two others, is still called Five-Ports. Only one village remains, bearing some traces of fortifications and old gates perched picturesquely on the cape. A long time ago, the sea came right up to the foundation; now it has retreated (and in other places, advanced) leaving a huge marsh filled with geese. The prettiest remain in the old city is the church which has evidently become Protestant, and heavily endowed besides. The choir is still standing, and in such a way that you can see the beginning of three now-disappeared naves on the present façade; the old church must have been extremely large. Of special note are the tombs of former lords and admirals depicted, on coats of mail, with their feet on a greyhound. All of that carries the vague scent of old days and melancholy. I don't know if this is the case with all things English or if we read into them because we know that we are in England. Yesterday, along with P. de Bélinay and M. Butterfield, curator of Hastings' museum, I went once again to the eastern cliffs to see the imprints of iguanodons and other animals. They weren't spectacular, but it was decided that workers should take out the most attractive group. Father Burdo even photographed the stone containing the imprints; I'll send a snapshot.

Meanwhile, a beautiful fox emerged from the crumbling rocks

and climbed steadily up the clay cliffs, proof that wildlife still exists here. Mr. Butterfield showed no special reaction to this; maybe foxes no longer exist when you take away the pack, the whips and the red-clad hunters.

Right now there are lots of pigeons. From my window I can see the gardener killing some of them in the woods at the foot of the house; I would rather see them fly away in peace.

Goodbye for now, dear parents. My love to you and Guiguite.

Pierre

8

Ore Place, Hastings
December 31 [1908]

Dear Father and Mother,

Right now (it's almost 6 P.M.) I'm thinking of all of you gathered in the living room at Clermont (by the glow of that well-known lighthouse). With all my heart I wish you a very Happy New Year. Our Lord will fill it with whatever He knows to be good for you and we can hope that it will be a good one from every perspective.

The most striking event during the past week was unquestionably the cold spell which moved in on the 28th, the heaviest blizzard (I don't guarantee the spelling) Hastings has seen in 28 years—so say the newspapers. In fact, even if the thermometer hadn't fallen below 9° (centigrade) there was an exceptional amount of snow for the area—around 20 centimeters. Yesterday, the countryside was gorgeous, and I indulged in the pleasure of going through the woods to take advantage of this particular kind which brings back some far-distant memories. I don't think I've seen a good amount of snow since Laval (and that day

Albéric came to see me). It was a dry cold, a cloudless sky and there was a bit of fog, all of which tinted the horizon dusty-rose. The English, on the contrary, were hunting, and gunfire could be heard from all around. The unfortunate rabbits seemed extremely frightened and dashed away in leaps and bounds that made them rather comical. From their tracks and the debris around their burrows, it was obvious that they were feeding on lichens.

Today came the thaw, and all around the house, clumps of snow and ice are falling off the roof, making a big racket.

We don't know too much here as yet about the tragedy at Messina; the first statistics in the English newspapers[1] seem fantastic. The catastrophe touches me, for I've had good views of the place from the steamer. Usually the great catastrophes occur in such obscure places that you cannot identify with them.

To clear up an ambiguity in my previous letter, I must tell Father that he is right to imagine a large crowd following the fox hunts. If this fact didn't appear in my description, blame it on the fact that from my observation point, I couldn't see the route where most of the hunters were located.

Our vacation ends tomorrow night; other than that, there's nothing special ahead—which reminds me; last year at this time, I was on the way to Miniah. Circumstances have changed since.

Goodbye, dear Father and Mother. Happy New Year and my love to all of you.

Pierre

1. An earthquake ravaged Messina (December, 1908).

9

Ore Place, Hastings
February 1 [1909]

Dear Father and Mother,

It made me happy to know that you enjoyed my article; I only regret that you had to borrow that issue of *Etudes*.[1] But yesterday, I patched up the oversight. Finally, I'm happy that this publication afforded the occasion of my "launching" and also that these first fruits were for the Blessed Virgin. It was considerate on her part and a favorable omen for me.

Besides this, I'm waiting for the Egyptian Institute to publish the Notes in which things "Teilhardian" play a role; but it's typical of the country and the Institute to take their time. While on the subject of Cairo: I recently received a very amiable letter from M. Couyat who must be in Sinai now.

1. *Etudes,* vol. 118 (January 20, 1909), 161–183: *Les miracles de Lourdes et les enquêtes canoniques* (Pierre Teilhard de Chardin). Several statements in this article bring to light certain characteristics of method and thought which will deepen later on. Thus follows the plan to show the "existence of a personal God by using a rigorously positive method" (164). Note too, the formula: "The hypothesis is the obedient clay which facts shape."

34

Nothing has happened here in Hastings during the past two weeks, except that the weather is fine enough regardless of the cold. We've had a few agreeable afternoons; the sun has been rather warm. I pounced on the chance to bring back a considerable number of small fossils, teeth and fragments of various shells from the cliffs. Evidently, Hastings isn't at all removed from social life as was Egypt, and you know that it's considered the Cannes of England.

Thank you, Father, for the article clipped from *Field* on hunting woodcocks in Sussex. I'm not familiar with the author. Eastbourne is relatively far from here (even though I can see it from my window) and as for Hastings, a scholastic's contact with the world at large is extremely limited.

I haven't seen the *Illustration* in which Abbot Moreux makes his predictions,[2] but one has to realize that in time, Sarcenat or le Rocquet will be a pleasant place filled with the charm of the sea.

It will amuse you to know that Ore's numerous robins are charming and friendly. One of them spends its days near a doorway and comes to eat from the hand, with a scrap of defiance; however: as soon as it takes a crumb, it flies away. When it doesn't get anything, it hops around, chirping; so impatient was it tonight that it flew around my hand before I could give it a crumb.

My love and prayers to you both. Best wishes to Uncle Joseph if he hasn't already left.

Pierre

2. Abbot Théophile Moreux (1867–1954), director of Bourges Observatory, and author of numerous works on popular astronomy.

10

Ore Place, Hastings
February 20 [*1909*]

Dear Father and Mother,

Here I am, a week late in writing to you, which won't fail to vex Mother. Blame it on Father Chauvin[1] who spent the past few days here. Like so many others here, I had to deliver a sermon in his honor; it really required preparation: hence, my silence. Fortunately, beside the sermons, the above-mentioned visit offered us the occasion for additional walks, and they coincided with wonderful weather: a bit cold, without rain, and a very beautiful sky besides. Within a week, I found the means to spend at least six hours in the woods, really the best way for me to relax. What's more, new fossils are comparatively plentiful, and in some cases, I'm beginning to have a better collection than the Hastings museum. Speaking of this, the curator favored me with a little account he published about a book which is by no means small. Dated 1703, its aim is to provide a "probable solution" to

1. The Reverend Louis Chauvin, provincial superior of the Lyons Jesuits (see *Letters from Egypt,* letter 33).

the problem of bird emigration. According to the author, birds retreat to the moon (!!) a trip which must require about sixty days. They live on reserves which they use up slowly. Because of things in the atmosphere which distract them, they're almost always hypnotized, etc.—The curator concluded his account with the wise remark that the ornithologists of tomorrow will laugh at today's ideas. Nevertheless, I hope that they will have less cause to laugh.

Last Tuesday, the novices from St. Leonard's came for a visit (St. Leonard's is about ¾ of an hour away from Ore)[2] and I met a young man by the name of Vimal du Monteil[3] of the Vimal family from Constantinople. He remembered having met Albéric over there. There were a few of Joseph's friends among the novices.

The visit ended with a football match where, happily, for the sake of their honor and despite their advanced age, the theologians emerged the conquerors.

I don't think I told you, but, among other things, we're studying Hebrew. For many, alas myself included, it's just a formality which means attending classes twice a week. Nevertheless, the fruit of my last class was the etymology of a word which would interest Father; it's the word "échec" (failure). The expression in Persian, "ech-cheikh mat," meant: the sheik, or the king, is dead. That is also the source of that game.[4]

At this time, your Centrals must be at home; I keep telling myself to write to them. And what will Yéyé do without his hunting?

2. See letter 11.
3. Henri Vimal du Monteil, S.J., airplane pilot who died in the field of honor (1889–1918).
4. Chess. —Tr.

A week ago I saw some storks in formation, or birds which were very similar. For the time being, there are millions of starlings. Thanks to careful treatment, the robins are more lovable; they need training as they show an amount of natural defiance.

Goodbye for now, dear Father and Mother. My love to you, as well as to Guiguite and the boys, if they are still at home. My prayers are for all of you.

Pierre

11

Dear Father and Mother,

The postal strike seems to be over, allowing this letter to arrive without delay; beside, I haven't noticed any difficulty with my correspondence. Your news has arrived regularly. It is reported that a number of people were traveling from Paris to London to guarantee some sort of communication; they carried the letters with them. For two weeks, Hastings was quite surprised by a new snowfall and an invasion of cars. The snow came right after my last letter and didn't stay as long as the last two falls. But there was enough to whiten the whole countryside for two or three days. Since then, we've been in rain and fog and you wouldn't guess it was Spring except for the crocus, snowdrops and narcissus which seem to be the English flowers.

The cars have been here for a week, about four hundred of them bringing a regiment from London. It was a military exercise for coastal defense, combined with the car dealer's advertising campaign. The newspapers must have played it up; seeing that the English are very proud of successful business ventures, they are probably trying to console themselves for their more debatable success in aeronautics. Personally, I didn't see the cars, as they came on a class day. The novices from St. Leonard's[1] were given permission for a special walk to come watch; but here, we've had to bear the burden of being serious people. Last week, if I had had a bit more cunning or presence of mind, I would have caught a beautiful pheasant which was slipping through the low bushes hardly a metre away. As it was in the cliffs, I was all thumbs; but I was also missing a good dog like they have at Sarcenat, the kind that's ready to throttle anything that runs.

Here we are, ten days away from Palm Sunday, which means the end of classes for the second semester. To finish off, eight days from now, on Saturday, I am to take the negative side in a scholastic debate.[2] It's not too entertaining. Then there will be two weeks to devote to various other things—varied, that is, as much as the scholasticate allows.

Tomorrow marks the eighth year since I took vows. I will pray for all of you; I've already told you a number of times that the more the years go by, the happier I am at having chosen this way to spend them. It's always been true, and I owe it to you. I embrace you.

Pierre

1. See *Etablissements, op. cit.,* vol. 4. art. "Saint-Leonard-on-Sea" (L. Rosette). There, in Sussex County, the Jesuit noviciate was housed in 1901. On certain feast days, the novices and theologians would get together at Ore Place.
2. This sort of debate took place each semester in front of all the professors and students of the scholasticate. See letter 33.

12

Ore Place, Hastings
April 26 '09

Dear Father and Mother,

I'm writing to you during some magnificent weather which came after a spell of small storms launched Easter Monday. Vacation held enough beautiful days to be pleasant; and now, here we are, into the last semester. Exams will finish it off at the end of July; they are preceded by a month of review; so there are only two short months of classes left.

Nothing exciting happened during vacation; and since my partner was absent, I couldn't get in any geology. I might add that this week, I caught up; among other things of value to me, I dug up a megalosaur's tooth, which is quite a rare find here. For want of places to dig on Easter Thursday, I went to two pretty parks which are more or less buried in the woods. One was enlivened by children playing under the watchful eye of a governess, which reminded me of my youth, —and what's more, it must have been a good place for hunting, judging by the branch-cluttered paths (sign of a pheasant brood) and ermine and weasel traps. Nearby hung a dead ermine.

Spring isn't too far along here and the large trees are barely green. The undergrowth alone is pretty, covered as it is by white windflowers.

You can imagine that the East has caused much talk here: Cairo, a bit because of the archaeological congress, but especially Turkey. I don't think our missionaries have been harmed, not even in Adana. But a young Father whose whole family belongs to the Armenian Committee has had some tense moments of anxiety. His brother in Constantinople was expressly followed to be murdered and only escaped with great difficulty. The rest of his family is in Adana and he hasn't received word from them yet.[1]

I've mentioned that the pheasants here are presently giving

1. Between 1894 and 1896 the Armenians had already been massacred in Turkey, and other massacres had taken place in 1905 in Russian Armenia. Between April 14 and April 17, 1909, new, more localized massacres occurred in Adana, capital of Silicia, having a population of 30,000 Armenians out of 70,000. They were to have gone back between April 25 and April 28. The French Jesuits from the Lyons Province had a residence and college (St. Paul) where they were helped by some Marist brothers; the Sisters of St. Joseph from Lyons had a boarding school, an orphanage, a dispensary and the beginnings of a hospital, all of which were burned to the ground.

It is known that between 1915 and 1918 more than a million Armenians perished in the Ottoman Empire under orders from Constantinople. In his April 22, 1939, speech to the military leaders of the Third Reich, Hitler announced his orders concerning the Polish population; he added: "Who still talks today about the extermination of the Armenians?" See *Etudes: Bulletin des Missions* by A. Brou, vol. 147 (April, 1916), 232. Aram Andonian, *Documents officiels concernant les massacres Arméniens,* (Paris, 1920).

The international review, *Missi,* (Lyons, Brussels) devoted its #4 issue in 1965 to: "Armenia and the Armenians."

their meadows a treatment which Auvergne ignores, if I'm not mistaken. They comb them carefully by dragging pine branches.

Another important event for England: the football season closes Saturday in London with the big final match. They tell the story that an Englishman from Hastings once wanted to go to this event and found 22! people in his compartment.

Faithful to local custom, we too, are going to interrupt our games.

Goodbye, dear Father and Mother. All my love to you. I will especially remember you on May 1st.

Pierre

13

Dear Father and Mother,

Once again, I'm a bit late in writing to you; and you might blame that on the post office—but your letters have arrived here on time. For the past two weeks, we've had magnificent weather which let down only today to the great joy of the farmers who needed the rain. Before that, especially on May 1st, there were some sudden snowfalls; they could be seen passing over the countryside without blocking the sun, a phenomenon which produced some attractive lighting effects.

Now the Spring has really come although the oaks are always greenish yellow, and the ashes absolutely black. The garden is filled with an incalculable number of little thrushes who don't have tails yet and who hop around in families behind their mother, trying to catch worms. Another blessing these beautiful days is to catch glimpses of the sea with its vessels. Thanks to the distance from Hastings, the boats take the short cut and pass by very closely. So, since the beginning of the week, from our windows, we have successively admired a large, five-masted schooner, and then a gigantic steamer owned by Lloyd, Germany. With the naked eye, and better, with glasses carefully made from a cardboard tube and two lenses from a pair of opera glasses, you can count the smoke stacks easily.

Last week, on a very beautiful day, I visited Rye, a pretty little Norman town built on a promontory across from Winchelsea, which I discussed in November. The countryside was gayer than in the Autumn. On the way, we stopped at Kamber-Castle, an old place fallen to ruin, located in the middle of a field separating the two towns mentioned above. There stands an old dungeon in an enclosure, the whole thing isolated in a marshy pasture. On the way back, we made numerous detours across beautifully wooded valleys. That same day, we asked directions at least ten times in a row from different people on how to find a quarry; they must have looked on us with bewilderment.

We've received some news about Adana. Nothing happened to the Fathers, but our house was burned and all those who had taken refuge there were killed. Scenes of unbelievable savagery took place there; it seems that Beirut and Damascus had the order to massacre.

In Beirut, the Moslems weren't found to be strong enough; in Damascus the vali had the courage to disobey.

I didn't read H. Bremond's article which Father mentioned but I've allowed myself to say that Newman admirer though he is,[1] the author exaggerates the role of the heart in Pascal.[2] As for

1. Henri Bremond had published some articles on Newman, collected in *L'Inquiétude religieuse,* three volumes of translated text (1905–1906) and in 1906, *Newman, essai de biographie psychologique.*
2. Article on "La conversion de Pascal," collected by the author in *L'Inquiétude religieuse,* 2nd edition, 1909, pp. 7–42.

M. Arminjon,[3] I knew he was in Cairo, but I hadn't thought that he was Albéric's old friend; I could have seen him easily. A year ago, M. Fourtan offered me his press card to go to the opening of the railroad at Khargeh; but it was impossible to accept.

Goodbye, dear Father and Mother. My love to you and Guiguite. I won't forget you Sunday on Our Lady's feast. May she and those who are close to her protect the family.

Pierre

3. A former student at Mongré, M. Pierre Arminjon was a professor at the school of Khedivial Law in Cairo. See *Etudes,* vol. 113 (November, 1907), 484, the analysis of his book: *L'enseignement, la doctrine et la vie dans les Universités musulmanes d'Egypte* (Joseph Burnichon).

14

Dear Father and Mother,

Right now, I imagine that you must have discovered all that Spring freshness which has passed through Vialles. Except for a storm here which lasted a few days, and sprinkled the country-side, we continue to have beautiful weather which makes England quite tolerable. We're now on vacation for Pentecost. It will only be four days, but the year isn't too long now.

To have more courage to finish it out, I'm going to spend all day tomorrow at Eastbourne where the chalky cliffs have taunted me for the past nine months: I see them on the horizon from my window. My next letter will no doubt contain an account of the trip. In the past two weeks, I've become acquainted with Charles Dawson,[1] a geologist in the area. It happened under

1. Charles Dawson, notary and amateur geologist, not to be confused with the famous geologist, John Dawson (1820–1899). See Claude Cuénot, *Pierre Teilhard de Chardin* (Baltimore, 1965), which gives the facts about the "Piltdown Man." The present collection of letters simply gives a few references to it. See *Letters from Paris* (New York, 1967), letter 32, notes.

amusing circumstances. While visiting a quarry close by, we were surprised to see the "manager" take on an understanding attitude when we discussed fossils with him. He had just discovered an enormous pelvis bone from an iguanodon and was very anxious to talk about it. I knew then that it was almost a whole iguanodon being found piece by piece, and the fragments (you could say crumbs, for I wonder how they can be recognized) are piling up one by one in a crate destined for the British Museum. Mr. Dawson always arrived when we were on the grounds and immediately, he would come over to us full of joy and say, "Geologist?" He lives on the Newhaven side, but can render us many services. At least we will have someone to call when the pieces are too large for us to handle.

Speaking about geology, in honor of the Teilhardi, I'm going to send you the reprint of a study on sea urchins in Miniah. These reprints were brought to me yesterday by a man straight from Cairo, one of my best friends, M. Georgiadès; he is the representative at the International Congress of Chemistry in London, and took advantage of a day off to come to see me here. It gave me a strange feeling no longer to be talking with him in his laboratory in Cairo, or in Holy Family's colonnade. Naturally, he filled me in on people and things over there.

It seems that the repression of Cairo's little riot (over the press) was highly comical. The demonstrators were mostly cabmen, boot blacks, muleteers who, upon seeing the policemen charge, fled via all the free exits.

Fire hoses were used effectively. It seems that the firemen took advantage of the circumstances to amuse themselves at the expense of the innocent. One unfortunate donkey-driver took refuge behind an overturned cart which streams from the pumps had dislodged, and he tried hopelessly to keep himself sheltered while his donkey was showered mercilessly. It seems to be extremely warm over there. To think that I lament the 35° average; only by taste, for the climate here suits me well.

My love to you, Father and Mother. I won't fail to remember you in my prayers to the Sacred Heart this month.

Pierre

15

Ore Place, Hastings
July 1, 1909

My dear Mother,

As you are wondering why the letter, I'm writing to wish you a happy birthday and I think that I've rarely ever had more of an occasion, as Our Lord has asked you for considerable sacrifices lately. After Aunt Louise, to whom you probably said endless goodbyes, there is Françoise who must have told you the big news of her assignment to the missions.[1] I didn't mention it in my letter to Father, as I didn't know if you had told him yet. But I can already tell you how much I share your sacrifice. Our Lord

1. Françoise had just written to Pierre: "During the month of the Sacred Heart, and on His feast day, came the fulfillment of my most ardent desires. At a time when I no longer dared hope for it, Our Lord, in all His goodness offered me . . . a mission assignment to China. To tell you that I accepted, after having prayed with all my heart, is useless. You do understand and there is only enough room in my heart to acknowledge it. How good Our Lord is to me! I've never understood Him better! The less I deserved this immense grace, all the more do I find Him generous for having granted it to me. The matter is completely decided and I am to leave Amiens at the end of July. I will announce the departure to Mother myself in a few days: I know she will make the sacrifice in a holy way."

was very kind to let her tell you in person. So she was able to answer all your questions; you saw how happy she was, and all of that must have helped to soften the blow. But poor Father must have really suffered; though to tell the truth, the sacrifice won't be more complete than the one which has been made. And then, when you come right down to it, you must be proud and happy that Our Lord takes one of your children so completely. It's proof that He is blessing the trouble that you've taken to bring them up solely for Him; and in His example, is a powerful safeguard for the boys. As for Guiguite, she does love the Sacred Heart and has already learned enough to give Him everything He wanted, so that I'm not worried how she will have received the news. I'll try to write again when I know that you have all received the news, officially.

It made me happy to hear that Guiguite was going to Lourdes; I suppose the idea of a trip along with the pilgrimage must cause you some apprehension; but the Blessed Virgin will protect you and she will be moved by the way you are going to her, with all the others, like the poor and the needy.

And now, my dear little Mother, I can only repeat how much I will be praying for you on the 4th. I will ask Our Lord to make you love His will uniquely and above all things; the coming years will pass as quickly as the last, especially as the past ten, and finally, the only thing remaining will be the consolation of having given Him what he requested. Happy are we from whom He demands much.

My love to you and Guiguite.

Pierre

16

Ore Place, Hastings
July 1, 1909

Dear Father,

As I wrote to Mother for her birthday, I'm sending you a personal letter as is customary. On the off chance, I've begun to dig up information on Angers. My sources are old enough, but I could, if you so wish, supplement them more accurately through a prospectus: on the whole, it requires the will to work; the majority of young people think mainly of amusing themselves and represent an uneven range of ability. For the time being, I'm under the impression that Joseph would do well not to go there until he develops a serious enough taste for the kind of studies awaiting him. He will probably receive the best advice in Antoing[1] where he should be well-known.

1. See *Etablissements, op. cit.,* vol. 1, art. "Antoing" (Pierre Delattre). There, six kilometers away from Tournai, Belgium, is the College of the Sacred Heart (1901–1918), directed by the Jesuits from Champagne. It screened the preparatory classes for the "Grandes Ecoles." Along with Charles de Gaulle, Joseph Teilhard de Chardin entered the Advanced School of Agriculture (associated with the Catholic University at Angers) in Oc-

I wasn't surprised at the bad weather that ravaged your hay-fields. The last two weeks here were still worse than the two previous, cold, rainy and without a really beautiful day. Still and all, we too have our hayfields, mediocre grasses where all kinds of birds thrive. The day before yesterday an angry farmer cut it all down and at least one rabbit along with it, which the agitated man put under his coat, rather hastily. For the scholastics, it was the biggest amusement of the day. Moreover, yesterday, four submarines came to sell the people of Hastings on the advantages of levying taxes for the fleet. They stayed to be admired for a day; needless to state, whether our glasses were working or not.

Last week a funny thing happened to me; while we were chatting with the curator of the museum here, we innocently told him about meeting up with Mr. Dawson[2] and about the iguanodon in the quarry. Did he change color: to have an iguanodon in his collection has been one of his dreams and we have to tell him that they are just about to take one out almost from under his very nose! What's more, Mr. Dawson belongs to the scientific society in Hastings; how more sinister could his conduct be? "I grow wild," he said. We wrote to Mr. Dawson to warn him of our indiscretion, and he answered us with a very friendly letter, but still smacking of someone who smells gold and the halls of the British Museum behind him, and who lets his scorn for Hastings and its museum break through. He declares that the people of Hastings would only ruin the skeletons if they tried to keep them, and I think he's right.

tober 1909. See R. Guilloux, *La formation d'une élite rurale* (Angers, 1923).

2. See letter 14.

As for other things, we are deep in review for exams. It doesn't seem as bad to me as the veterans painted it. We still have a while before exams.

My love to you, dear Father.

Pierre

17

Dear Father,

In writing to you last time, I didn't mention a word about Françoise's departure because I was afraid the letter would come before the news itself. But I owe you a word about it now. I myself was no less surprised than you; though I'm used to seeing how departures are made for the missions, the sudden decision was no surprise. I also knew that Françoise wanted to go, and I can tell you that I understand her; but along with you, I thought that she would be assigned to direct some house in France. You have to believe that there is a place in a foreign land where she is needed just for that.

There is a deep sorrow for all of you, as it has always been consoling to know that you could go to see someone whenever you wanted, even if it only rarely materialized. So, I want to tell you that you are more in my thoughts these days because of this. Really, I believe that you must be proud of your daughter. Françoise is doing something beautiful there, greatly honoring the family which already owes her for more than one blessing. I think Albéric would have been very moved, but also proud; and as for her other brothers, there's a very convincing lesson on the necessity of making one's life useful.

My poor Father, you have made all kinds of sacrifice on behalf of your children; but that has always been to give something to God; at that price comes the confidence that you are in His favor. In the end, you will be happy that He has taken so much from you and won't consider anything else more advantageous.

Also, it seems that events like these bring us closer together and make us love because the family seems more beautiful. There's the advantage that Shanghai is almost a familiar country to me. Since I'm close to the Fathers from Paris, I hear them speak about it constantly, and I know almost all the young people from over there; some of them are my best friends. At least you can be sure that the Little Sisters in China are not isolated or lost.

My love to you as well as to Mother and the boys.

Pierre

18

Dear Father and Mother,

This letter will reach you as you spend the last few days with Françoise.[1] I don't have to tell you how much I'm united to you in this separation which comes after so many others, and which almost doubles the sacrifice you have made of Our Little Sister. I only ask Our Lord to help all of you give that courageously. Later on you will be happy to have given so much.

Like yourselves, I was angered over Gonzague's failure. The news came quickly thanks to some former professors from Marneffe who are here. This angering incident, coming as it does on a string of other painful events, must have seemed very disagreeable to you. As for Gonzague, I think that he can learn a lot during the extra three months he is required to take. I remember that for my license, it seemed that I doubled my knowledge. And then, it must be admitted that the choice of a

1. Before leaving for China, Françoise was allowed to say goodbye to her family, on account of her sister Marguérite's bad health.

French assignment was unwise. . . . Finally, I advise him and wish him to have a good vacation just the same.

I think I'm going to be able to provide Joseph with some definite information on Angers; when it comes, I'll send it to you. Meantime, I've learned that the students there are more or less divided into two categories, one containing bright young people who don't like to work. In the other, which is less smart, it is easy for a person to work seriously. That is already something.

We continue to have deplorable weather (since June 2); these last days we've had sun. Thanks to a violent west wind which must have really bothered planes from Boulogne, their owners haven't been up to amusing the public for awhile.

Nevertheless, Tuesday brought good weather which coincided with an excursion; I made it to one quarry and to lots of woods, the best relaxation to my mind. In a park, I was surprised to see ostriches walking around free as deer; I couldn't see what species they were, but most of them were gray and small.

Thursday, I took my new friend, Dr. Dawson, the geologist[2] to the cliffs to show him the iguanodon tracks. So high was the tide, and so violent the wind, that the expedition was heroic. Mr. Dawson isn't very used to the rocks, and both Father de Bélinay and I had to help him over the obstacles. I had all the trouble in the world rescuing his hat from the ditch. Finally, it was decided not to remove the prints that weren't clear enough. On the contrary for the British Museum's collection, he asked us for some teeth from a small crocodile which hadn't been seen yet on the terrain where we are. I found a supply of them Tuesday.

2. See letters 14 and 16 above.

With all that going on, we are also in exams; I will have finished Friday night. Afterwards comes a two-week vacation and then retreat.

My love to you both along with Guiguite and the boys.

Pierre

19

Ore Place, Hastings
August 7, 1909

Dear Father and Mother,

This letter comes to you during our vacation which has been unfolding gaily, blessed as it is by beautiful weather which seems to have returned expressly for it. All the English are just as happy as we about this favor from heaven. Beaches along the coast show signs of great happiness. This week we didn't go out too much; we had lots of company: one night in particular brought all the young ones from St. Leonard's and Canterbury[1] together and that made quite a large crowd. I don't think I've ever seen so many Jesuits at the same time. The drawback lies in the fact that it's hard to get to know anyone in such a crowd. There in the midst we formed a group of elders which made us realize that a long time has passed since Aix and Jersey.

What's more, we're going to see them again: today we were invited to St. Leonard, and Thursday to Canterbury. I really

1. See *Etablissements, op. cit.,* vol. 1, art. "Cantorbéry" (Charles Mitshe). The novices and minor seminarians of the Parisian province lived there.

appreciate this last friendly gesture, as it will take me to see an interesting corner of England. Next Sunday, before going into retreat, I'll tell you about it as well as a geological expedition I'm thinking of taking Monday to Folkestone.

Last Thursday, we had a lovely walk near here to the old castle in Bodiam.[2] Some took a carriage like the ones you see in *Graphic* or in Dicken's novels; at Rye, along with the remainder, I took a little gas boat which goes up the Rother to Bodiam itself. The Rother looks like a huge, winding ditch bordered by rushes; under the wide-eyed gaze of a number of little cows and bulls you wind your way through pastures bordered by wooded hillsides. There were peewits and herons which were almost fearless. Bodiam is a large square castle flanked by eight towers (a round one at each of the four corners—and four square, one placed in the middle of each side), surrounded by large moats which are, in turn, circled by great oak trees. The moats were full of water-lilies in full bloom, and the castle's gray stones stood out against the oaks with great clarity. Those of us from Auvergne are hardly accustomed to seeing such a strong castle at the bottom of a valley; you have to admit that Bodiam is one place to have seen. The Old England must have been interesting, and a person can still feel it very near.

You must be enjoying your vacation in Sarcenat. You saw general Pelletier who came to put his son into Bexill and who willingly took it upon himself to give you news.

In the same mail, I'm sending Joseph some information which he should have. Here enclosed you will find part of a letter written by one of my friends to someone from Angers who

2. To the north of Hastings in Sussex; built in the fourteenth century.

knows the University well but who isn't interested; the answers were put in the margins.

Goodbye, dear Father and Mother. My love to you as well as to Guiguite and the boys. I think Françoise must be on the Red Sea by now. Not without feeling, I tell myself that she is seeing the Arab mountains where I left part of my heart. All the best.

Pierre

P.S. I was certainly disturbed to hear the news about Just. I hope that the next letter will be more reassuring.[3]

3. See letters 23 and 24.

20

Dear Father and Mother,

Just a word or two, as I promised, before going on retreat. This last week of vacation went very well, like the one before, and the weather is warmer yet: it hit about 25°. The days have been filled with things which I will tell you about. Monday, I went to Folkestone which I only recognized by its station. The town impressed me; quite hilly with old sectors reminiscent of Hastings, and small torturously winding streets which make you think of rue de Port (minus the height, and the darkness of the houses); all in all, it is very elegant; I haven't gone to the western coast yet, where the "Parade" and fashionable beach are located. Coming for geology, I went to the beach where the chalky cliffs begin, and continued up to Dover where the breakwater is clearly visible. Our efforts were rewarded: under the chalk is a layer of clay full of fossils, ammonites mostly (they're not too well-known) which are very interesting and quite pretty; they have changed into pyrite, and a layer of mother-of-pearl which gives them a bronze tint and a marvellous luster. The sea pushes them up and rolls them like pebbles; you only have to collect them. Our example caught on and soon a group of bathers started collecting too, but exercising a more dubious differentiation. France was hidden by fog, but at least the steamer from Boulogne was visible. I came away with the impression of a very gay life there, and still smelling of privet hedges in bloom; this last sensation in particular takes me back to Sarcenat and a familiar place.

Tuesday, I made it to Canterbury. Hardly had I arrived when I rushed over and carefully inspected the cathedral, with the exception of the rear choir and crypt. At the same time, I had a good look at the Black Prince's[1] coat of mail. I was disagreeably surprised to see the profusion of funeral plaques commemorating the heroes from India or South Africa. The nave is beginning to look like a marble warehouse and it's hard to determine its function. The Office takes place in the choir which is closed off for the occasion. From the nave, I assisted at morning offices. First-come was an especially distinguished clergyman wearing black gaiters and a many-tasselled top-hat. After awhile, he left the sacristy preceded by a certain number of cantors or deans wearing very original costumes; there were also some nicely dressed choir boys: deep purple robes with great white collars. I noticed that these same youngsters were poorly grouped (I probably noticed that because of my own former duties in Cairo). I only saw the procession; afterwards, I had to be satisfied with listening to hymns. As far as I'm qualified to judge in such matters, the music and voices are marvellous, which is the very least

1. Edward, the Black Prince (1442-1483) and King, son of Richard of York.

consideration for a church of such importance.[2] Afterward, I went to our house in Canterbury, Father du Lac's[3] former college, where the juniorate and the house of renewal, formerly at Laval and Bon-Secours, are now located. The house is very large, but all in red brick which isn't too attractive. By contrast, the park is huge: one third woods, one third meadow and one third field with an abundance of farm machinery and beautiful cows, a stable lit by acetylene torches, but unassuming enough not to deserve Father's roof. From the house you can see Canterbury and the cathedral beyond the meadows. It was an agreeable stay but didn't compare to Ore: it's humid and the atmosphere is heavy; you are drowned in the midst of stifling hills. There is a very beautiful row of great cedar trees. The furnishings, statues and tableaux etc. at the juniorate took me back to Laval and to the first days in Jersey. Moreover, I met a young priest, Father Duranton.[4] The first thing, I asked him if he were from the coast of Ambert; but he replied that he is from near Gannat. As at Auvergnat, I saw young Father du Bouchet[5] (please ignore the

2. It was a custom among young French Jesuits who were passing through Canterbury or living there (Hales Place) to go to hear the organ at the Cathedral. Father Teilhard certainly knew the great poem of one of his old confreres, Father Victor Poucel (1872–1953), composed on such an occasion. This poem, *Office du soir,* has been included in a posthumous volume, *Présence divine,* the edition prepared by Victor Fontoynont and Jean Rimaud, S.J., presentation by Jean Rimaud (X. Mappus, Le Puy-Lyons-Paris, 1960).

3. Father Stanislas du Lac (1835–1909), educator and preacher, was rector of the college of Sainte-Marie in Canterbury. He was connected with the Dreyfus affair, since he had dealings with General de Boisdeffre.

4. Father Louis Duranton (1883–1954), professor of history at St. Joseph College in Avignon for a long time.

5. Rev. Joseph du Bouchet became Apostolic Prefect of the new Jesuit mission in Tchad (1947) after having been Provincial of Lyons.

spelling) whom Father Vimal had introduced as his very own.

In my last letter, I forgot to mention that in the cliffs I killed a huge viper which had six little ones inside. It seems to be a rare thing in England and maybe *Field* would be happy to publicize it.

To answer Father's question: Bodiam is authentic from way back and completely uninhabited; but for the time being, I'll ignore the details of its history.

Enclosed is a post card which chanced to by-pass me yesterday; it shows Bodiam. A bit to the right of the round tower at the right, you will notice two racks for drying hops, something which is typical of this country.

Goodbye for now. My love to you and to the boys.

One thing I failed to mention—I will probably go to Jersey in September to do some mineralogy. But I'll tell you about it between now and then. You won't be forgotten during the eight days. You know that the retreat will end with ordination on the 24th. My love to you.

Pierre

21

Hôtel et Restaurant Continental
L. Cottin
25, Oxford Street.

Dear Father and Mother,

Maybe you are surprised at the heading on this letter, as my last one didn't say anything about leaving Ore so quickly. To tell the truth, I'm on my way to Jersey, and am presently trying to fill up a four-hour wait in Southampton; not far from port, I found a humble restaurant run by a kind of Breton. So I didn't have to pull out my still-rudimentary English; I'm writing to you from there.

To start from the beginning, our retreat finished exactly a week ago. Tuesday was ordination; Bishop Amigo from London officiated.[1] The ceremony was very beautiful, and a considerable

1. Bishop Amigo, Bishop of Southwark, ordained more than five hundred Jesuit seminarians who had taken refuge in England. See letter 54, notes.

number were ordained. I think if my poor mother had been here, she would have been very jealous; but there are only two years to go. You know that the parents attend the ordination, then the first Mass on the following day. It is very moving to see each new priest celebrating before members of his family. On the following days, the house is really in an uproar because of the departures, and you know why I'm not looking forward to the fourth year, at least not for the time being. Two Fathers left for Shanghai, one of whom is Father Froc, Director of the famous observatory and also extraordinary confessor for the Little Sisters; you can be sure I gave them a few messages for Françoise.[2]

To get back to me, I left Hastings this morning via excursion train, an inexpensive way to get to Rye on the Isle of Wight. The benefit of a daytime crossing was to let me see a good part of Southern England. The rest is pretty dull.

The prettiest moment is crossing the downs between East-bourne and Brighton. After that, the country is flat; you can't see the sea: only a green plain with brick houses all too often. Brighton itself appalled me: the rows of little houses seem longer than usual and when the sun shines on all these rows of identical, criss-crossing roofs, you'd think that the hills were covered with a shroud. The approaches to the beach must be lovely, but I didn't see them. A little before Chichester, you pass close enough to Arundel, but I didn't think of looking. The inlet at Ports-mouth is more impressive. You disembark at a port where the long gray shapes of the battleships stretch out: they're very amusing to look at. Little steamers provide constant service to Ryde; the passage lasts half an hour, crossing a path where you

2. About Father Froc, see letter 43, note 1.

can still see other armoured vessels, almost all of the same design, with four smoke stacks. At Ryde, Wight is extremely smart, but is missing the cliffs I would have liked (they're in the South and Southwest), and which I could have easily seen by train had I known the schedule more in advance. So, at Ryde, the coast ends in rolling landscape covered with villas whose grounds go down as far as the sea. That's where the Benedictines of Solesmes have settled, (if I'm not mistaken); it's also the home of the Bishop of Portsmouth on which Jersey depends. The town is very stylish and overlooks the sea; that's to tell you that the view is very beautiful. I arrived at noon and left at three for Southampton on another little steamer. The two-hour trip is very pretty. It passes Cowes where the grounds of princely estates reach as far as the water. You cruise past pretty yachts with long sails, the owner taking it easy in the back, the crew, dressed in white, gathered at the bow. Finally, as you arrive in Southampton, you pass a series of transatlantic ships, of all lines (Union-Castle, Lloyd, White Star, etc.). I don't think I ever saw the comparable in Marseille. From the middle of all that, you have to ferret out the steamer for Jersey. We leave at midnight and arrive at 8 a.m. with a stop at Guernesey. I will write to you without too much delay. I'm there for the whole of September. So write to me at Maison St.-Louis.

Goodbye for now. My love to you as well as to the boys and Guiguite. May the boys have a good hunt and may Guiguite not be too tired from her trip to Vialles. I thank her for the last of Joseph's work. The *Fer à Cheval* pleased me especially. My love to you.

Pierre

22

Ore Place, Hastings
October 10, '09

Dear Father and Mother,

Here we are again. Classes resumed last week;[1] it seems as though Jersey is already a long time past, and yet my last letter was dated from there which goes to show that I still have to tell you about my return trip. Before leaving, I was able to take an important trip to the north in marvellous weather. Notably, I saw "Devil's Hole" which I think Mother visited since my last trip there; the trophy for the day wasn't in the world of minerals, just an alga which hadn't been noted in Jersey before. As I was telling you, I returned through Weymouth. The crossing is a bit shorter and is made by excellent steamers with two red smoke stacks which Gonzague would have recognized. In Guernesey, we lost considerable time loading baskets of grapes; so I busied

1. During this and the following two years, Father Teilhard had the following professors: in dogmatic theology, Fathers Xavier Le Bachelet, Stéphane Harent, Marcel Chossat; in sacred Church history, Father de la Servière; in canon law, Father Choupin; in sacred scripture, Fathers Albert Condamin and Alfred Durand.

70

myself with the view of St. Pierre and by watching the manoeuvres of a school of jelly fish, gray with brown stripes. Although a bit overcast, the weather was calm. Having left at 8:30 in the morning, we saw England around 4. Coming in, we passed Portland's inlet at the left; it's made up of a high rocky plateau, meeting the ground in a pebble embankment.

Weymouth is a pretty little seaside town with a tiny harbor and a "parade." I even saw a noble highlander (at least I think he was) wearing the complete Scottish regalia under his coat. In a paternal way, he was watching the antics of two little urchins, but still kept that lordly air. Especially admirable was the Isle of Portland. Over and above interest in its earth strata, which are very rich in fossils and the like, there is the seemingly absolute wildness. I got there late enough just as the sun was setting in a vast expanse of gray sea; the top of the isle is almost desert and is pitted by old quarries: under a foggy sky, the whole landscape looks like something in the nordic regions. Contrary to what you could believe, they don't make cement in Portland any more; from time immemorial, they have only used the very hard, chalky banks to any great measure.

The trip from Weymouth to London let me see a bit of England from the inside. The line goes up almost to Bristol. You don't go by any famous towns, but the uneven ground is remarkably green. From Reading, the freshness turns to marsh and the place seems to be populated by water fowl. At the same time, the sky gets dark and, the approach to London turned out to be dismal that day. The Huntley-Palmer plants (in Reading) and Scott emulsion plants didn't brighten up the countryside; then there were these rows and rows of identical brick houses as far as the eye could see.

In London, I only saw a bit of the street and the subway which carried me underneath the capital's most famous places. My on-the-spot impressions are restricted to St. Paul's seen in the fog from a cab, and to a young student from Eton, who was wearing a top hat and short jacket. It's weak, but maybe I shall have the chance to do better in your company or that of one of my brothers.

Here, I found that the number of scholastics has increased still more; outstanding, there are some especially nice Americans (two of whom look like Taft[2]) who are the greatest people in the world. One of them even promised to become a geology colleague. The country is beginning to take on an autumn look which I really like. Finally, the beginning of this year has seemed infinitely more gentle than the last, when I had to put Cairo out of my mind. Did you see any of the aurora borealis on September 26th? In Jersey, we only saw the end which looked like lilac clusters extended to the skytop.

Thank you for Françoise's last letters. I'll be careful with them and will make sure to return them. Tell Guiguite I won't delay in writing to her; I didn't have time at this point, but I won't forget. My love to you.

Pierre

P.S. Can you get me an address for Just?

2. William Howard Taft (1857–1930), President of the United States from 1908 to 1911.

23

Ore Place, Hastings
Oct. 24 [*'09*]

Dear Father and Mother,

Since my last letter, a heavy class schedule has rarely occasioned anything exciting. Outside of classes, time is spent waiting for a period of storms to end and nothing prevents it from continuing. Last night, an uncommonly violent wind blew in from the south. Calmed a bit though it may be, the sea is still heavy, judging from the white waves which rise before the steamship.

What you told me about Just, and especially his family, is very sad. I wrote to him; I think my letter will have arrived on time.[1] If God decidedly wishes to take him, that will make a good number of "departed" in the family and many feasts to celebrate on All Saint's Day. As every year, I will be more especially united to you that day and the following, in commemorating those who have left us.

But now to get back to Ore. We're in an annoyingly disagreeable period as far as the weather is concerned. I've rarely made

1. See letter 24.

such muddy trips as I did last week, which is quite the fault of my choice. These rainy periods have the advantage of putting me unmistakably on the track of quarries, thanks to the rutted trails. That's how I found a new one in the vicinity which has proven to be exceptionally rich in crocodile teeth.

As for other things, football has resumed with gusto and the new recruits look good, especially the Americans; these latter, however, need more training. Back home, it seems, they learn rugby, which must be quite a pastime for people like themselves.

Walking in Hastings, I was surprised to see a generous number of political posters concerning the newly proposed tax; accompanied by an explanatory word, they used such generally unfavorable symbols as a workman or peasant crushed under a heavy burden. Elsewhere, a large Englishman, wearing a belt inscribed with the name of the tax, and crying, "Help, Britons!", is being pushed to the edge of dizzying, chalky cliffs by an Italian, a German, an Austrian and a Russian. I didn't understand absolutely everything.

Speaking of posters, I don't think I mentioned two which I saw last time in Jersey. The first is like this: "Here animals are taken, dead or alive. J. Pestel. The most expensive are taken."

The second, which is nothing less than an ordinance, forbids anyone, no matter who, from keeping at home, live, "all harmful animals, insects, fungi or other pests liable to injure the fruits of the land."

And the expression comes back in a whole series of articles in the ordinance.

I received a note from R. du Buysson about some Chryses which I sent him from Jersey; he's truely a likable fellow. He tells me Mathilde is in Paris.

Goodbye to you both, for now. My love to you and to any of the boys who are with you.

Pierre

24

Dear Father and Mother,

Even though it was to be expected, notice of Just's death grieved me.[1] In the old days, when I spent my vacation with Albéric, Joseph and him, who would have thought that I would be the only one left, so soon. . . . Under similar circumstances, those who don't believe in a good and rational divine will which shall make up for everything, must really be unhappy; and yet we can believe that everything has happened for the best. After all, even though that may seem stern, God didn't give us life so that we could please ourselves, but in order that we serve Him in whatever pleases Him. I didn't forget you around All Saints'

1. See letters 19 and 23; also letter 41. Just de Lalaubie (1882–1908) was Pierre's cousin (his paternal grandmother was a Teilhard, a sister of Pierre's grandfather) and his friend from childhood (the Teilhard de Chardin's and the de Lalaubie's were neighbors in Clermont). Having studied at the School of Polytechnology, like his father, he became an officer. Just left the army to enter the French seminary in Rome. During the summer, he became seriously ill in France. His mother was the sister of Just de Bretenières, a martyr of Korea.

Day, nor on Loulou's anniversary. I'm happy that you could have your family there. Here, we ended up by having good weather with the cold. But the rains did their damage and the newspapers must have told you how we were flooded. In one day, 5 centimeters of water fell. The immediate result: large streams which wind through many valleys in Sussex rose to overflowing, turning pastures to lakes and drowning many sheep. This latter kind of disaster came from the flash floods which rose in just an hour during the night. It seems that Folkestone was so seriously flooded that homes were damaged inside; from this disaster, I learned how harmful a waterflow can be.

At least the flood offered the migrating ducks a sanctuary. I saw some flocks which were slightly wild. This year the geese seem rather abundant. We saw quite a few in the brushwood along the shore; they were probably headed for France.

Here, life continues calmly and studiously, broken by the growing mania for football, and by a trip to the crumbling cliffs. This latter outburst isn't too great after the last rains; I see a magnificent potato field (something akin to Carthelades) still in bloom in July, and a good corner of it is ready to extend to the sea.

Goodbye, dear Father and Mother. My love to you.

Pierre

25

Ore Place, Hastings
November 23, 1909

Dear Father and Mother,

Thank you for your fine last letters, as well as for Guiguite's. Since my last one, the most notable event has been the arrival of good weather which has stayed on. While they say that France is under a blanket of snow, we are having some wonderfully dry-cold days. They're lightly foggy but almost without clouds. Last week even brought an excursion with it, allowing me to enjoy the Autumn in Ashburnham. I hadn't been there for a year. This time, due to storms and a more advanced season, the hues of the beeches weren't as rich, but they were still lovely. I saw flocks of deer again and shaggy cows with long horns. Even the lanes seemed richly kept due, I suppose, to the presence of the lord. This seems to be hunting season and the unfortunate pheasants must be having their bad moments. Normanhurst's park (neighboring on Ashburnham and famous for its rhododendrons) was staked out with numbered rods. I didn't see any geese, just a tardy swallow. I noticed that I consistently keep forgetting to tell you about a new, but trivial decision which was made about our ordination. From now on, we shall not be ordained subdeacons at the end of 2 years, but rather, just a few months before the priesthood. So, I shall be a subdeacon, not this coming August, but 8 months later. Mother may feel let down, but there's no reason for it; I shall be a priest and maybe even a deacon just as soon as I would have been under the old system; as for the subdiaconate, it's an order which carries hardly any privileges with it. Let her tell herself more, that all these joys together will begin to be heaped on me in no more than 18 months from now.

I finish this letter at the end of an exquisite walk near a foggy sea, lit by a low, red sun; on days like that, I always regret that Ore isn't at the tip of Scotland, or on the Island. It's getting colder and colder here, but always stays beautiful; starving robins are becoming a touching, familiar sight.

Goodbye, dear Father and Mother. My love to you both.

Pierre

26

Ore Place, Hastings
December 22, 1909

Dear Father,

According to custom, I am wishing you a very merry Christmas. Once more, following the ordinary rite, I can promise you an affectionate remembrance at my midnight Mass; it will be very nice. Waiting on Saturday, I will ask Our Lord more than ever to bless this year for you and to let you enjoy your children —even those furthest away. I don't have to keep letting you know how much I always love you. Your two soldiers will be home to brighten up Christmas. I'm happy about that. If only Angers would be generous towards its students.

I'm writing to you at the end of one of the four big scholastic debates which mark the school year. Today's debate was quite outstanding. We had the advantage of putting almost all of this semester's material to use. No less appreciable, it marks the definitive beginning of vacation. Classes won't resume again until January 2nd. May the weather in between be accommodating. It doesn't look that way.

Last week we had a first snowfall which lasted a day; today there's a storm with rain and fog. Also, as soon as you leave Hastings, there's an indescribable mud, almost as horrid as in Belgium, say people from Marneffe. At the same time, the cliffs are crumbling beautifully, but nothing significant has been uncovered with the exception of some pretty fern and ordinary pine cone impressions. England is preparing to celebrate Christmas in a dignified way. For the past month in the city, you could see posters telling when you should mail letters so that they would arrive when you wanted in all the English-speaking countries. The food merchants are starting to display almost repulsive pyramids of fowl in shops decorated with holly. Yesterday, it was touching to see groups of more or less poor children celebrating a bit beforehand, noses glued to the windows of all the bakeries. These poor little ones can't have too soft a life; in the long rows of identical little houses which make up Hastings' outskirts, there often seems to be real destitution.

Another sign of Christmas is the appearance of musicians (lone singers armed with accordian, or small orchestras like the ones at "Cinq-Ports") who begin to play right under the windows at Ore Place, in the evening darkness. They managed to grind out the Marseillaise for us. I only fear that our doorkeeper encourages the remnants of such a naïve and confident tradition as little as possible.

Adieu, Father. My love to you, as well as to Mother and the boys.

Pierre

81

27

Ore Place, Hastings
January 16, 1910

Dear Father,

Having written to Mother thanking her for her New Year's gift, I'm addressing my ordinary letter to you, albeit slightly a bit late perhaps. It follows our renewal of vows this morning, preceded by a triduum. I didn't neglect to pray again that God would bless this year for you and your children; you know very well that I am always perfectly happy on the path which I have taken and which you have allowed me to follow. As for our Little

1. On October 20, 1909, Françoise wrote to her father: "One of our benefactors here belongs to a great Chinese family, and personally instructs our aged. He really has a regal air and not one of our European gentlemen could greet the Mother Superior with more politeness and graciousness . . . Our good, aged Chinese have all my sympathy; that surprises you, but, it's true that they all have good faces. The little old ladies sometimes argue and cry a bit, but many are really sweet, and all of them are generally easy to manage . . . I thank Mother for her good prayers for the Chinese. I've put myself to it resolutely; dialects abound . . . I hope to be really into it soon. Tell Pierre that Father de la Servière gave me his letter which will have its answer January 1."

On December 27, she wrote to her mother: "My vocation's beautiful

82

Sister in China, she seems to be very content;[1] in a letter which came this morning, she tells me that she found everything she wanted in her Chinese quarter of Shanghai. Our satisfaction must have cost you dearly, but God will reward you for that.

I suppose the same mail pouch must have also brought you news from China. In this case, you will have still more information than I; my letter holds hardly any news other than that perfect contentment is springing out and affection for the Chinese as well.

To finish my outside news, my collections from Egypt continue to be classified little by little. I received a report describing the fossilized starfish which I collected near the pyramids: there are four new kinds, 3 new genera and a "Metapaster (!!) Teilhardi." These starfish certainly represent one of my best finds from antiquity; they all come from a four square metre place; two were found side by side, and another, the day before my departure.

M. de Joannis paid me tribute with an "Emblemma Teilhardi" (a small gray night moth dotted with black and white and which lives on mimosa).

Maybe you know that Robert du Buysson won a prize of 1500 francs for his report on the Egyptian Chrysidides. He answered my congratulations with a card which had also been signed by Paul and Emmanuel du R.

---

days in France held their shadow, and if, with all my might, I kept renouncing the attraction which was tugging at me, to go further off, I couldn't erase it, for God was really calling me to do just that. Today, too, I must thank Our Lord and the Blessed Virgin, for I don't desire anything else in this world if not that they preserve this happiness for me and grant me the strength to live and die in this land of China, in the midst of our poor Pagans." (See letter 37.)

At the British Museum, someone recognized the shells (similar to our Planorbis) which I had collected in October as something no one had discovered in the area before.

We are right in the middle of elections. For the borough of Hastings, elections took place yesterday; the results aren't out yet (*a fortiori* for England, where elections extend into several weeks) but the Tory candidate is favored. His name is du Cros and he sells automobiles, a profession which gives him marked advantages. Last Spring, it was he who provided a good number of cars which brought the London regiment here. It was also his blue and white cars (unionist colors; the liberals add red) which went all through the town looking for home votes. They say there were the typical spectacles: for example, a woman dressed in blue and wearing a white hat, was leading a little girl dressed in white and wearing a blue hat; she was pushing a plush bear in a blue and white carriage which is all the rage this year.

Better still: Mr. du Cros' children were riding ponies and carrying this slogan: "Vote again for daddy." Two years ago, when they were younger and perhaps richer in child-grace, they were driven in a car with the slogan "Vote for papa." It's the same principle as in the *Suitors*.

To the bitter end, the posters caused a furor, and some of them were almost hateful; the unionists could afford artistic things (chain gangs without work, men made jobless through foreign competition, John Bull crushed under a hail of imported products) while the liberals beamed inexhaustibly in the sumptuous clothing of Peers, appearing on the back of a wolf. Speaking of posters, I noticed two clever ideas: a Peer complacently looking at himself in a mirror with this motto, "He only represents himself"; and a Robinson Crusoe looking dejectedly at the deserted

84

sea; he's standing next to a hut labelled "made at home" or some such thing.

Since the first of the year, we've had mild temperatures, but very bad weather; it rains almost every day or else it brings thick fog; for all practical purposes, you can't see the sea any more. When talking about the elections, I forgot to tell you that Father Rector was visited by a delegation of ladies decked patriotically in white and blue, who had come to win over votes. It seemed that a popular rumor circulated that we were going to come down from Ore Place in a body of around five hundred (!!) to make the conservative candidate win. It's rather amusing. Wherever we go, it's written that we appear as an occult power. Admittedly, our customs could be amazing at times.

Goodbye, for now, Father. My love to you.

Pierre

28

Ore Place, Hastings
February 16, 1910

Dear Father and Mother,

Winter continues to be deplorably rainy; since the beginning of the month it's rained 13 out of 15 days, and this has made the country like a sponge—without including the eroding cliffs all along the shore; at least this last fact bears the advantage of assuring me some work. Despite the rain, the meadows are not turning green yet.

On the last Sunday before Lent, ordination of deacons took place, a beautiful ceremony, but not to be compared to that for the priesthood. It seems to be confirmed that a year from now, we will be ordained subdeacons and two days later, deacons. As usual, Bishop Amigo was his gay self, but deadpan; he didn't miss the chance to joke with the Americans. Last Thursday, we were given an extremely interesting conference by one of my old friends from Jersey, Father Bernard, a missionary in Alaska who is now doing his Third Year at Canterbury. His district, which is as large as Belgium, goes from the Bering Strait to the

Arctic Ocean. He lives almost completely alone with the miners and Eskimos. Half the time he travels, making about 100 kilometers by dog sled, dependent on his dog team's sense of smell and their caprices. The cold reached –60°. Judging by the photographs, his dogs are very friendly, even though it seems that they sometimes grow as ferocious as wolves. Some of them show an ability to get their bearings and lead dogs are chosen from among these. Often, one has to rely on their instinct. To recognize their future leaders, they make the young dogs run near a team; those who have the "gift" place themselves up with the current leader. The Eskimos make good Christians and are remarkably upright for the most part.

Isolated on an islet in the Bering Strait is a group to which the missionary can't come. The chief spontaneously took it upon himself to call the people together every Sunday for prayer. (It seems that these people's sorrow over not having a priest moved him to pity.) The miners are equally good people, or at least, they are moved by what people do for them. They gave Father Bernard some nuggets and a solid gold rosary (it seems that the Holy Father received a similar one) which one of them had brought from I don't know how many kilometers away. For the time being, Father Bernard is traveling through France to collect money for a church and to find some missionaries if possible. He's sure that despite the isolation, his life is inviting. But there is this to consider: you can only do good in the place where God wants you to be, and I have many reasons to believe that I won't be allowed to even want to go up there.

Aside from that, there's nothing new here; the loss of the *Général-Chanzy* moved us deeply; Father de Paris who was going to give Lenten talks in Algiers, was on board.

Goodbye for now; my love to you and Guiguite as well. May this Lent without the Josephs and the Mareschaux not seem too long to you.

Pierre

29

Dear Father and Mother,

Three days ago marked the anniversary of my departure and I can still see it as though I were there. Had I stayed at home, I think we would have seen much more of each other, but it would have been over by now; whereas, this way, we can offer God eleven years of separation wanted only because of Him. Don't you think it's all for the best and that we must be very happy about it?

I'm happy to think that your boys will be back with you for vacation. Here too, we're having vacation; there's good weather even though it's a bit cold in the morning. The shrubs are turning green and the edges of the stream are being filled with Pilewort, Chrysosplenium, and a very unique little flower whose blossoms are grouped in pyramids of 5's, the adoxa moschatella, I believe. I'm not sure if it's found in Auvergne. If I'm so taken up with botany, it's because I met my friend, de Bellaing this year. We had gone looking for algae in Jersey, and his present fervent interest is in mosses. I only went back to him to get a general appreciation of paleobotany and to stir up enthusiasm to dig in the clay cliffs at Fairlight; meanwhile, this winter we collected a good number of ferns and pine cones.

This year, they've done a series of plantings in Ore's garden; I especially appreciated a skirt of rhododendrons which I would never otherwise see in their splendor.

Among the trees which are now standing and which date back to the old grounds, there is a very curious one: a hybrid juniper and thuya in which the characteristics of the two species subsist absolutely intact but as if they were blended. The branches are part juniper, part thuya, and you can even see that the shoots which are thuya for a few centimeters, become juniper. Does Father know if this is widespread and artificially reproducible in horticulture?

William de Jerphanion just won a 500 franc prize from the Geographic Society for a map of Armenia which he drew up himself. For the time being, he's in Paris.

My love to you both, Father and Mother.

Pierre

30

Dear Father and Mother,

You must be happy to have received news from Françoise at last, and happier still that she continues to be content over there. I really believe that under no circumstances could you have had the joy of seeing her as satisfied. Why were there no acceptable candidates in Clermont, so that all the constituents had to be called? They recruited from Lyons, and since a number of colleagues were named, there was a little exodus of people yesterday leaving Ore to go and vote. In the northern departments, and in Belgium, the committees call all their people regularly. They even assure me that a Father came all the way back from Constantinople to vote.

Evidently, we aren't that high up yet at the Center; Mother surely agrees with this. I wish Charles of France luck. Did I tell you that two of my comrades from Mongré are around Grenoble? One is almost the same age as Gabriel.

While you have a cold gray sky, the weather here has been

mild, slightly rainy, and has some good stretches of sun; also, things are growing noticeably; the sloe-trees on the cliffs are all white, and the underbrush is completely carpeted with anemone. Nothing equals the present color of the larch trees. There are many clusters in the Sussex woods. The swallows and cuckoos have been back for a week; Father Johnston, the ornithologist, has a lot to do to keep up with the new arrivals.

In the same mail, I'm sending Guiguite a description of a few Egyptian butterflies. Believe me, I ask myself if I will ever give science many other new finds in this genre. Theology makes me think about a lot of things and I'm beginning to perceive that there are so many other questions, less appealing, maybe, but more vital than the sciences, that I wonder if I shall not be side-tracked one day or another, unless they tell me not to do them, which is a strong possibility.

Today, on the feast of St. George, the football season winds up: but all the same, we are continuing until May 1st. After that, I'll have the time to go walking.

For the feast of Joan of Arc, we welcomed the novices from St. Leonard, which gave me the chance to see du Bouchet again. Father de Moré[1] is here for awhile (from Marneffe). He's been better for the past two years; but I don't see when he will be able to do his theology.

Goodbye, dear parents. My best to Olivier when you see him. My love and prayers.

Pierre

1. Father Charles de Moré-Pontgibaud (1881–1959). Author of *Du fini à l'infini, Collection Théologie* (Paris, 1957). He was Dean of the Faculty of Theology at Angers.

31

Ore Place, Hastings
May 8, 1910

Dear Father and Mother,

Guiguite's state of health was a joyful surprise to me, given that such an improvement is so perceptible. Whatever the extraordinary degree of these repeated recoveries, it is difficult not to see God's very special hand; we can't express too much confidence in Him or acknowledge Him enough. You must be happy to see Guiguite up and around, and she must be enjoying Sarcenat if the Spring has finally arrived.

Here, the biggest news is, of course, the King's death. We are far from Hastings here, and Hastings itself is enough of a "hole" so that echoes coming to Ore are very weak. It's easy to see that the English are very touched. I suppose that in France, they must admittedly be mourning Edward VII.[1]

As father predicted, we were proud of Paulhan's success; even passers-by in the streets announced it to us. For this occasion, the

1. Edward VII, king of Great Britain and Ireland (1841–1910).

Daily Mail had a good piece. Speaking about Manchester's citizens watching the arrival of the French candidate (though their sympathies were for White) whom they received, nonetheless, with enthusiasm, it passed this monumental judgment: "They forgot that they were English people looking for an English boy's victory: they became sportsmen." All the same, our ancestors would have been very astonished at this new way of triumphing over the English.

This week, I received a voluminous *Mémoire* published at the expense of the Egyptian Institute by M. Pallary, my friend from Oran; it's a catalogue of land and fresh water shell life found between here and Egypt. My collections have an important place and there's even a "Sphaerium Teilhardi."

Among all the things I collected there, the only one left to classify is an important series of pliocene shells; their search took up the whole Autumn of my last year in Cairo; but I don't know when I'll have time to do it.

To elaborate on the reflections sketched in my last letter on a like subject, I think Father is completely right in considering pure theory as one of the most active elements in making the world go round. So, I haven't tried to deny it. But I perceive that beside strictly scientific objects which have occupied my mind until now, there's a whole collection of human questions which constitute a field of studies just as lively no less fraught with problems. . . . It doesn't keep me from making a good wager that my first future destination will be to join a group of physical scientists.

As for the weather, the month of May made a bad entrance; we aren't emerging from a storm, accompanied by rain and squalls, or by anything for that matter—that's almost worse, since nothing could have been more unwelcome for those beautiful fresh leaves than a violent wind and cold.

Unfortunately, a boat from Hastings sank.

My love to you both.

Pierre

32

My dear little Mother,

I received your good letter of the 20th in which you speak of Orcival and your new curé. I never went there; we were supposed to have gone one day with Albéric; then we missed our train, and the occasion to go never returned. Thank you for having prayed for me and my priesthood: that is coming up so soon. . . . I understand your disappointment over Gonzague. I don't know what Father Rougane will have answered; from everything you tell me, I would tend to think that there's a matter of scruples. We have to ask the Sacred Heart to break the ice and make Himself loved a bit more warmly by this poor Gonzague, who, no doubt, would be so happy if he knew how to do it. Tell Guiguite to remind him, without seeming to do so, that I would really like him to answer as he promised. Since I'm on the subject of Guiguite, say that I recommend that she not overwork herself. I know that is very difficult, but let her read and meditate a little on what Our Lord might say to her as if to St. Martha (in Luke, Ch. 10, verses 41–42); let her try to moderate herself in doing her little bit, and without getting upset if she doesn't succeed; otherwise, the remedy would be worse than the ill.

I'm very happy that you have finally found a curé after your own heart; I guess Father is going to be highly amused to see you and your lady friends filling him in.

Since I won't be writing to you before June, this is the time to tell you that I shall be praying to the Sacred Heart for you, the family, your work, and I know that you will do the same for me.

Let's never forget that the greatest pleasure we can give Him is to have confidence in Him—and may our confidence in Him never be greater and truer than when we cannot hook our hope onto anything human. Then, He alone remains; one hopes in Him alone. Then may He make us understand that His will is the only absolutely necessary and precious thing here below, . . . that which stays and takes the place of everything else. Then doesn't that will seem better, when you think that it comes from the Sacred Heart? What won't a person accept in the knowledge that it is He who is acting in us.[1]

Goodbye, my dear little Mother. All my love to you. Don't worry about boring me in talking about everything that claims your attention.

Your child,
Pierre

1. See *La prière du Père Teilhard de Chardin,* by Henri de Lubac (Paris, 1964), in particular, pp. 13–18; in *La mystique et les mystiques* (Collectif Ravier), see pp. 887–890, by J. A. Cuttat, on the presence of God in Père Teilhard de Chardin (Desclée de Brouwer, 1965).

33

Dear Father and Mother,

Here I am after almost three weeks of silence.

To start off with the most recent news, and the most agreeable to me, Saturday's ceremony is over. Everything went, if not brilliantly, at least in a respectable way, and now I find myself more or less relaxed. If it interests you, the current style for theological debates runs as follows: the negative side must uphold six propositions; two specially appointed examiners challenge him on two propositions in the morning and evening as well—at the end, those who wish, from among the "*ornatissima adstantium corona*" may also join in. The rite hasn't changed a bit for centuries, and everything goes on in Latin, naturally. I must reiterate once again that my teaching days didn't have a favorable affect on my ease in speaking this language, much less for writing a thesis; it is reminiscent of preparing for my license.

To finish off the topic of studies, here we are, almost at the end of our classes; they will finish on the 21st, which is also the day we renew our vows; after that come reviews which last until July 21.

The end of Spring continues to be beautiful, almost too warm on some days and very humid. Every morning, there is fog; showers and storms are not wanting, all of which helps the hay immensely. As the countryside here is practically all meadows or woods, the region is now a very rich green. When I wrote last time, Halley's comet was still visible; it couldn't have been more beautiful here than what Father saw in Sarcenat, partly because of the long twilight and the full moon. One of my old students in Cairo wrote me that they could see a very good tail.

On the feast of the Sacred Heart, we had a procession in the garden. It's something new, and for the first time, strictly a private affair; only the novices from St. Leonard came. I think that the doors will open wider in time. At least we had marvelous weather.

The beautiful days have multiplied the swallows; they aren't nesting along our roof yet, but they're flying around the house with cries that undeniably remind me of Sarcenat—minus the noise of the water jets.

Right now, we're being read the concise history of the Jesuits in France which is about to be published.[1] Auvergne has a beautiful place in the beginning, thanks to Mgr. Duprat.[2]

1. Henri Fouqueray, S.J., *Histoire de la Compagnie de Jésus en France des origines à la suppression* (1528–1762), 5 vols. (Paris, 1910–1925); vol. 1, *Les origines et les premières luttes* (1528–1575).

2. Guillaume du Prat (1507–1560), son of Antoin du Prat, chancellor of France (who became archbishop of Sens and then cardinal), Thomas du Prat's nephew, successor in 1529 as bishop of Clermont. Thanks to him, the first college of the Company of Jesus in France was founded at Billom in 1556. See Fouqueray, *op. cit.,* pp. 150–194. *Etablissements, op. cit.,* vol. 1, art. "Billom" (M. Dousse).

Yesterday, they told us how the Huguenot minister from Maringes ran away when Father Edmond Auger[3] went to him alone. The country must have been beautiful then. In the *Bulletin de la Société Française de Minéralogie* (the February, 1910 issue) there was an article on beryl (common emerald) from the Olliergue vicinity. It could be purely a study of crystals, but there may also be details about deposits and locales, and these latter may well be near Murat. I saw another viper in the cliffs, but I couldn't kill it; there are decidedly more in England than I thought.

Goodbye, dear Father and Mother. My love to you. Thanks, Mother, for Françoise's letters; I'll keep them carefully for her. I will be thinking of her pilgrimage on the 19th.

Of course, I'm praying hard for all of you this month.

Pierre

---

3. Fouqueray, *op. cit.* p. 348. *Etablissements, op. cit.,* vol. 5, p. 254.

34

Dear Father and Mother,

Gonzague's success made me so happy. The news came before Mother's letter, thanks to echoes from Marneffe. He who is concerned must be greatly soothed and really in the mood to take a vacation. If only he could see clearly into the preparation for his future, and with God's help, take the direction best-suited for him. It would really help if he were to find a career he would really like, or at least one which would truly motivate him to accomplish something good. I guess that must worry you quite a bit, and I pray that you will happen upon the right thing; I hope that happier days will shine upon Father's hayfields; but you'll have to have better weather than we. Even without a lot of rain, we are only emerging today from the cold and fog; it didn't seem to bother the farmers too much; they had to content themselves with stacking half-dry hay. During July, it was more or less sad.

Review time is progressing to the point of being considered

finished, for all practical purposes. Only there are numerous candidates and I'm still only in second year, from which it follows that I shall hardly be free before the 25th. Except for us, the others are on vacation; for these last few days, we've seen young Americans passing by on their way back from Belgium. Their confreres brought them here (they don't look like them at all; they're small and have faces like children) or else they came to see famous Ore. One of them managed to go through Reims, and came away with a flattering impression of it; not even in America had he seen so many cars. I had the pleasure of seeing another visitor who had come up; it was Father Lammens[1] whom you had seen at Sarcenat two years ago. He has just become associated with the new Biblical Institute which Pius X has founded in Rome. The Holy Father shows it extraordinary favor.[2] In the absence of news from Italy, which he still hardly knows, he gave us some about Cairo. He has just come from there; it seems that things are going from bad to worse, as nationalist agitation deprives the country of its security. In itself, the party isn't so dreadful, but it has infiltrated all the government schools which guarantees trouble for a long time to come. Otherwise, it is plainly Moslem, to the point that authentic nationals, outside the Copts, have been excluded.

Last week, we had a day to walk; I went to the woods bordering Ashburnham; they are very beautiful at this time. Little pheasants were not lacking and there were still more little rab-

1. See *Letters from Egypt,* letter 65.
2. The Pontifical Biblical Institute was created in Rome by Father Léopold Fonck, S.J., an Austrian (1865–1930) in charge. On this appointment and others, see M. Blondel and A. Valensin, *Correspondance,* vol. 2 (1957), pp. 351–352.

bits: I even found one of them under a stone I overturned; but I was so surprised to find it there, that I let it escape.

My love to you both, dear parents.

Pierre

35

Ore Place, Hastings
August 29, 1910

Dear Father and Mother,

My departure this year is just as hectic as it was last year when I went to Jersey; tomorrow, I'm going to Holland. I'll be going through London, Harwich, Anvers and will probably arrive Wednesday at the latest. Without delay, I'll write you about the trip; meantime, you can address your letters to "Kastel Gemert, Noord-Brabant, Holland."[1]

Much has happened since my last letter. First, retreat, which for not having a wealth of stories to recount, still marks one of the highspots of the year. During that time, I didn't neglect to pray for all of you, and I would like to have emerged a better Jesuit than when I entered. Then, at the end, came the ordination of priests; it was especially beautiful because there were so many—about thirty or so. During the ceremony, I couldn't help

1. See *Etablissements, op. cit.,* vol. 2, art. "Gemert" (Pierre Delattre). In the old castle in Northern Brabant (Holland) the Scholasticate of Philosophy and Science of Vals was located, by order of the law of 1901.

but think that next year would be my turn, and that you will be there among the parents. That brings me closer to the priesthood, along with saying each day: In a year, I shall be saying Mass. Pray that Our Lord finds me worthy, as much as one can be, given similar material.

There was a great number of guests: around 120 people. Hastings' citizens were filled with admiration; these are the days which can't make Ore Place mount high enough in their esteem.

A young priest from Paris stopped here on his way to Shanghai; even though it isn't the quickest way, I shan't miss out on giving him a word for Françoise.

Goodbye, dear Father and Mother; until the next letter, my love to you as well as to the boys and Guiguite.

Pierre

36

Dear Father and Mother,

Here I am. I arrived yesterday, safe and sound after the best trip in the world. As I wrote you, I left via London, where I stayed a good half day. At least this time, I wasn't restricted to going through underground, as I was last year on my way back from Jersey; although the tubes did me good service, I now have a better idea of the city. To begin, one of my friends whom I met over there, insisted on taking me through the Japanese Exposition (doubtlessly something which I wouldn't have done by myself and without getting lost). About half of it is a huge village fair with an abundance of dizzying amusements: the flip-flap, the scenic railway where the passengers obviously enjoy themselves, sheets of moving metal made to look like waves; little cars move in circles, etc. . . . The exhibits are more serious; beside the pleasure of meeting and talking with the Japanese, you see many typically Japanese things which are really remarkable: replicas of costumes and postures, with emphasis on the military,

going from the ferocious warriors of the VIII century, to officers
from the Russian war; there are also women dressed in European
garb, numerous laquered reliefs splendidly inlaid with mother-
of-pearl representing birds, porcelain vases whose value was evi-
dent by the amount of pounds sterling shown on the price tag,
patient miniatures representing the main cities in Japan, etc. I
must admit that I wasn't too impressed. It's more a bazaar. The
industrial and scientific aspect was represented by mineral samples, bigger than they were beautiful, seismographs, corals, a
collection of land and sea animals (without mentioning the fish
with two tails). The English section was about the most interesting; the house of Armstrong displayed a large cannon, and a
lathe which made shaved steel chips as large as a finger; we saw
airplanes and many spinning machines; the *Daily Telegraph* was
displaying its presses and linotype machines in full operation.
New Zealand has a pretty pavilion. I forgot the genuine material
from the Shakleton expedition which showed a venerable wear
and tear. Leaving all that behind, I was plunged into the calm
of South-Kensington where the natural history collections are. I
only saw the paleontology collections, but those were of keen
interest to me; I even saw one of the samples I saw in Hastings;
it was in one of the display cases. We stopped for a break at
"Lyons" just across from Westminster; from there, an 8 o'clock
bus took me across the bustling Strand; the sky provided me
with a beautiful evening; connections with the Continent were
carefully assured; the train stops at the Harwich pier right across
from the steamer; one only has to get on board. When I went
up on the bridge around six in the morning, after a peaceful
night, we were coming into Flessing; a huge sun was rising
over the Scheldt. The rise of the river is monotonous enough;

with a string of buoys as a guide, you coast between two low green shore lines, on gray water from which huge, muddy banks emerge. For amusement, you cut off freshly painted barges, or cruise by enormous cargo ships from all countries; these were making their way slowly. A large transatlantic arriving from New York gave us the same pleasure. As the steamer approaches Southern Anvers you skirt all the docks; the great steamers stand in review, a spectacle not to be looked down upon.

Until Wednesday morning, I profited from the generous hospitality offered by the Fathers at the College. What impression Father had of Anvers four years ago, I no longer remember. As for me, I have been amazed: the main street leaving the luxurious buildings of the central station, and from Meir, to wind up at the Flemish houses surrounding the Cathedral attracted me especially. As for the Cathedral itself, I admired the outside especially. Rubens' paintings were not on display, and as in other places, the museum's admission fee made me draw back. I left without seeing any Flemish art, much to my regret. To console myself, I visited the zoo and gave special attention to the great anteaters, the pheasants, the crowned pigeons and finally, the reptiles. There was also a very sociable orangutang; greatly annoyed by the people gaping at it, the animal went to lie down under a blanket on a little wooden bed.

Finally, Wednesday at 10, I boarded a train whose cars had "Amsterdam" written on them, and entered Holland through Rosendaal. Getting around isn't too easy, and it's hard to know if questions should be asked in French, German or English to be understood. When all is said and done, French always stood by me. I found that I had arrived on the queen's birthday: everything was decked out with orange and the national colors, even the people; important people wore rosettes; little boys wore capes and little girls wore sashes. I went through places named Breda, Tillbury, Eindhoven, and across a country of infinite moors covered as far as the eye could see with red heather in bloom, or woods of thick pines. Gemert is in the midst of a marshland, and doubtlessly I could describe it in more detail next time. To come to the point which I'm discussing, you have to use a rustic little steam-operated tram which takes you for an hour along the canals and across the little villages filled with blond, happy-faced children vying with each other to wave. Kasteel Gemert, as the name indicates, is an old castle which once housed Teuton knights. Large moats filled with pikes surround the house, and the old dungeon has a stork nest which, unfortunately, the storks left last month. Everything is very green, the climate mild, for the time being, and there's an air of deep calm; a person feels relaxed in the country, and the scholastics here lead the real life of men of the field; it's neither like Ore nor Jersey.

They gave a charming welcome, and I've already begun to busy myself in the biology laboratory. In my next letter, I will speak to you at length about the life here.

Yesterday, Father's first letter postmarked "Murol" came. Regarding the decree on First Communion,[1] they say that a Belgian priest in Anvers has already put it into practise; a "liberal" newspaper judged that there was everything to gain, as children must be freed from the catechism just as quickly. Personally, I think

1. The Decree *Quam singulari* of the Congregation of Sacraments, published August 8, 1910; the first of eight promulgated rules stated: "The age of discretion for both communion and confession is around the age of seven, i.e., the age of reason. From this time, one has the obligation to satisfy the double precept of confession and communion."

that the practice will soften many of the inconveniences so easy to foresee. On arrival here, I heard a quick reading of the Letter on Sillon. It will cause pain to a great many people, and many others, no doubt, would like to see social works condemned there; it seems to me that Pius X could hardly do otherwise, or say better. I would be curious to see the impression it made in France, as well as the Sillonists'[2] attitude. Goodbye, dear Father and Mother. My love to you as well as to the boys and Guiguite; I'm sorry to hear that she's not as well as before. I'll try to write to her next time. I pray for you all.

Pierre

2. The "Sillon" was condemned on August 25, 1910, by the encyclical *Notre charge apostolique* addressed to the Bishop of France. See Blondel-Valensin, *Correspondance,* vol. 2 (1957), pp. 175–177. H. Daniel-Rops, *Fight for God* (New York, 1966), see chapter V, "Pius X and 'God's Interests.'"

37

Dear Father and Mother,

It will soon be a week since my return to Ore; so, it's about time to write to you about what happened on the way back. Above all, I want to tell you something you scarcely doubt, that is, that yesterday, the 27th, I thought of everyone for a long time and prayed for them in memory of our dear Albéric. As Mother wrote me, each year brings us closer to him, and also, each year means a generous supply of merits deserved by your sacrifices. Just think, a year from today, God willing, I shall be able to offer Mass in his honor.

Imagine, when I arrived home, there was almost fresh news about Françoise. Shortly before leaving Shanghai, on his way back from China, via Siberia, Father de la Servière[1] saw her and told me all sorts of good things. The summer hasn't tired her out at all; she is really happy and is beginning to progress in

1. Father Joseph de la Servière, Doctor of Letters, professor of Church history first at Ore, then in China.

Chinese. It seems that along with the Sisters of the Presentation, the Little Sisters are on their way to becoming one of the adornments of the mission. The elderly abound all over China, so much so that Mgr. Paris[2] is preparing to care for all the members of his diocese—and they would really like to open a house in Nankin.

As for other things, vocations promise to be numerous, and it is all the more beautiful, seeing that they cannot be received as yet, due to prejudices and customs, or because they belong to the best families. Father de la Servière confessed that the Sisters shame the missionaries by the way they work from morning until night in all that heat, while they have all they can do to get around in the midday heat.

Now let's come back to Gemert. I left it Monday, the 19th and not without great regret; the evening before, I spent some exquisitely calm time in the pine woods of Peel; over there, where the wind is so gentle, the autumn leaves take on some rare tints; I can still see a whole grove of red oaks. Moreover, I left behind a good number of friends made during those three weeks, and I don't know if I shall ever see that big family, lost in a corner of Holland, again. That day, after changing trains three times (the last was at Landen on the Liege line), I arrived in Louvain. I entered Belgium through Akel, a very unattractive side; the sectors of Limbourg neighboring the frontier (which are soon to become an important coal-mining region) still have great moors: but after that, there is only the promontory of cultivated ground.

2. Bishop Prosper Paris, S.J. (1864–1931) founded or promoted countless charitable institutions (St. Mary's Hospital) and teaching institutions (Aurore University).

For my day-and-a-half stay in Louvain, one of my classmates and best friends from Ore these past two years, awaited me;[3] thanks to him, I found myself at home. Louvain is a little old city, wavering inside its ancient ramparts hidden away under the grass; only students from its important Catholic university live there. In virtue of this, it leaves a person with a penetrating, rather sad, sense of respect. The Hotel de Ville is designed like a shrine; the cathedral has a tower which has been crumbling since the death of Juste-Lipse; on each corner of the street, a person runs into one of the forty existing colleges, many of which serve one of the multiple branches of the university on the spot.

Right near our house, where the Belgian Fathers have their philosophy and theology, rises the tower where Jansenius composed the *Augustinus*. Besides this remembrance worthy to interest a Jesuit, I found many others: our church has St. John Berchmans' heart and Lessius' tomb; you can even see a farm, once the chartreuse where Canisius and Bl. Lefèvre[4] are said to have received hospitality. Unfortunately, I couldn't get to Diest. Besides these old remnants, swarm as many French as there are Belgian religious communities; their convents crown almost all the heights surrounding the city; in 1834 . . . the Dutch army un-

3. Father Pierre Charles (1883–1954). See Jean Levie, S.J., *In Memoriam, le Père Pierre Charles, S.J.*, in the *Nouvelle Revue théologique*, vol. 76 (1954), pp. 254–273. In the encyclopedia *Catholicisme* (de Jacquemet), by U. Milliez (vol. 2, cols. 990–991). See, in connection with Father Teilhard, *Mémoires échangés entre M. Blondel et P. Teilhard de Chardin en décembre, 1919* (Bibliothèque des Archives de Philosophie, 1966), introduction.

4. See J. Broderick, S.J., *Saint Pierre Canisius,* translated and adapted from the English by J. Boulangé and A. Noché, preface by Joseph Lecler (Paris, Spes, 1956), 2 vols. Bl. Pierre Favre (alias LeFèvre), *Mémorial,* Collection *Christus,* no. 4 (Desclee de Brouwer, 1959).

fortunately and almost spontaneously routed the Belgian soldiers from there. I took advantage of the stay to meet many Fathers who are quite versed in either the physical or natural sciences.[5] Finally, on Wednesday morning, I took the Brussels motor-train. Before being quartered in the new St-Michel College, at the other end of the city, I went by Grande-Place, Ste-Gudule and the king's palace. Grande-Place by far enthused me the most; I also arranged to go by 3 times during my stay. Built in the new sector near Avenue de Tervueren, St-Michel College is huge, done in Flemish style, and too luxurious say many people; at least it houses the Bollandists.[6] I stayed there just for meals and over night. I spent the whole first evening, before going to the Exposition, looking at Cetacean fossils from Anvers, Mosasaurians from the chalk beds at Maestricht, and above all, the only herd of iguanodons in the world; these were found in Bernissart's pits (in the very same strata as at Hastings). At the Exposition, some barricades and wooden triumphal arches covered with green

5. Among them was, probably, Father Joseph Maréchal, S.J. (1878–1944), who taught biology and experimental psychology at Louvain until 1914 and who published various studies in natural history from 1903. He became known through his work in mystical psychology (1908) and in the philosophy of knowledge. Father Teilhard was always very receptive to his judgements. See Auguste Grégoire, S.J., *Le Père Joseph Maréchal*, in *Nouvelle Revue théologique*, vol. 67 (1945), pp. 695–703. *Mélanges Joseph Maréchal*, 2 vols. (1950): in the introduction of vol. 1, biography of Father André Hayen.

6. The Society of Bollandists, a group of several Belgian Jesuits dedicated to the editing and critical study of hagiographic texts of Christian tradition. Its founders in the seventeenth century were Héribert Rosweyde (d. 1629), Jean Bolland (d. 1665) Godefroid Henskens (d. 1681) and Daniel Van Papenbroek (d. 1715). The work has been carried on in our own time by Fathers Hippolyte Delehaye (d. 1941) and Paul Peeters (d. 1950). See Paul Peeters, *L'oeuvre des Bollandistes* (Brussels, 1942). *Figures bollandiennes contemporaines* (Brussels, 1948).

plants absolutely mask all vestiges of the fire which doesn't seem to have discouraged visitors, judging by the crowd. Coming there on business, I had to leave many nice things aside to go to see the extremely powerful radio station and the physics exhibit. The German section interested me especially, maybe because it is intact: but one has to confess that it isn't gay. Following the exotic pavillions, one more ridiculous than the next, it looms a massive, austere, slate-covered building. Tall Germans, with moustaches like the Kaiser, and wearing military dress guard the door. The inside throbs with colossal motors, besides which there are pianolas, mechanical violins and other interesting contraptions. When I answer Biel, I'll tell him about Zeiss' high-powered microscopes. What proved to be the most vivid impression of savagery and brutality, was to hear a tall German with a megaphone, praising the shells destined to be used by aviators. "That weighs 1 kg. and destroys a thirty metre radius. . . . Excellent against villages." There was a crowd of onlookers present to be petrified by this dismal charlatan.

Despite everything, what burned leaves an infamous gap; and then, there wasn't a single airplane to be displayed. Another highspot at Brussels, says the "Cinquantenaire" is an extraordinary exhibit of old Flemish paintings; unfortunately, it was expensive to see, and I didn't have the time, so I left Belgium without having seen a single beautiful painting—I really regret that.

To mention la Cambre woods, located near the Exposition, does Father know that the line separating Flemish-speaking districts from French-speaking districts marks the old skirt of a huge forest (la Cambre is only a vestige of it) which the Francs didn't dare invade?

Thursday morning, I left for Jette, which is only a half-hour's train ride from la Bourse; thanks to the night spent at St-Michel, I could fit in a visit to Aunt Louise. The convent was easy to find, and they gave me a welcome you can well imagine. Aunt Louise will have written Mother about it; she must have had to muster up some good will to say that her nephew was perfectly awake (considering the Bohemian life he'd been leading for several days), but I was very happy to see her. I really thought I was talking to Mother.

Of course, I went to pray near the tomb of Blessed Mother Barat; it's in a very beautiful, slim Gothic chapel with lovely pews and marvelous polished floors, the likes of which I've only seen at the Sacred Heart. We visited everything there was to see, admired the large grounds with their beautiful trees and large pond. There, around 2 o'clock, I had to say goodbye in order to catch the Anvers train. This time, I didn't stop; the car pulled up in front of the steamer. Just beyond the string of huge, transatlantic steamers, with their lighted portholes, I could pick out the cathedral's silhouette. The sea was still calmer than on the way over, and all I did was sleep until we reached Harwich on Friday at 5 A.M. I spent the day in London. Crossing the St. James section and the edges of Hyde Park on foot, I went slowly to South Kensington (so that I'd only arrive when it opened at 10). This time, I stopped at the Catholic cathedral which I found immense, rich, but a bit disconcerting at first glance. It's Byzantine (a wise choice, for it might have competed with Westminster)—the high spire is a square tower which ends in sort of a small cupola. The still-incomplete interior is to be thoroughly covered with mosaics and rare marbles. Two completed side chapels give the impression of unheard-of luxury. The English don't take money into account.

Leaving the natural history museums, I crossed Hyde Park and went into the British Museum where the ethnographic and antiquity collections alone remain. One of my friends from Ore works there; he took me through, but I went around so fast that I just saw the most interesting things, busts of Caesar, friezes from the Parthenon, Assyrian bas-reliefs, Rosetta stones, and finally, a few manuscripts. Then I took the train to Hastings; I was glad to be back. Now, I'm getting ready to pass my exam in moral theology, scheduled for next week; classes resume after that. We're having magnificent weather which has lasted since the end of August: also, the leaves are drying out and the dust is thick.

I forgot to tell you that I left Gemert 2 days before Father de la Vaissière[7] arrived; it seems that he is an older man and entered the noviciate two or three years ago. He's from Cantal and would have been a banker (?).

I suppose he's one of our cousins.

Goodbye for now, dear Father and Mother. My love to you both.

Pierre

7. Father Jules de la Vaissière (1863–1940), author of *La Pudeur instinctive* and *Eléments de psychologie expérimentale* (Paris, 1931).

117

38

Ore Place, Hastings
October 11, 1910

Dear Father and Mother,

Today I decided to settle my correspondence with Gabriel and Olivier, so that I don't have much time to spend on your letter. Besides, compared to September, the last two weeks are quite scanty as far as news is concerned. The most important is that I finally completed my moral theology exam, and by that very token, my required study of this subject. I say "required" because, in practice, I must continue studying it for a lifetime; but it's already a real pleasure not to have classes any more. From now on, I consider myself to be on the way to ending my theology studies. The glorious event of October 4th, was followed on the next day by the resumption of classes; we're still in that unrewarding stage from which a person feels he cannot extricate himself. As happens every year, our surroundings have fairly changed; there are fewer candidates and they include many from Marneffe whom the Molochs know well: Father de Chalain, Father de Vaumas, Father Le Jarriel. Besides this, the strange,

118

even exotic element, especially the Mexican, continues to cut a good image. There's one interesting character, a powerful and jovial German who is extremely well versed in knowledge about Indian palm trees; he seems to have studied them from all angles. I'm trying to get him interested in the fossilized flora found in the Hastings clay, but I'm afraid his generous size makes any exploring of the area impossible.

Up until now, we've been without any precise details about our Portuguese Fathers.[1] If the revolution gets the upper hand all over the country, we'll be receiving refugees here. One of the Portuguese Fathers I saw at Gemert assured me that the elections had been very good, but trumped up by the government! If at least the new regime would allow the Pope to act more independently there, there might be a good side to all this mess; for it seems that the clergy are really in need of reform.

In Auvergne, I think people will have been moved by the two Moranes' accident; it's decidedly more difficult to get to Puy-de-Dôme than to go through the Alps. Just the same, even for the more quiet people, flying seems to be a prime interest; as for me, I'm beginning to look forward to the time when I see a plane pass by. It's probably the thrill Michelin wants to give his fellow citizens when he flies around the cathedral.

To answer Father's question, it's possible that the tableaux he mentioned are still in the British Museum, at least if they haven't been taken to the National Gallery; it's only the Natural History exhibits that I've seen taken out.

1. Following the unpopular dictatorship of João Franco (1906–1908), the king of Portugal, Carlo I and his son were assassinated. The young king, Manuel II was exiled in 1910 and the provisory government of T. Brager was violently anticlerical.

When I learned that Landen[2] is only ¾ of an hour away from Marneffe, I almost regretted not having made this little detour to see a famous house. As for the king's palace in Brussels, there are still scaffolds against the front; it seems they're doing some sculptures.

Goodbye, dear Father and Mother; my love to you. I'm happy Mother's knee is better.

Pierre

2. A little Belgian village in the Province of Liège, where Father Teilhard had changed trains on his way to Louvain.

39

Dear Father and Mother,

Judging from the shower of hail from the south, the day before yesterday, you must really be snowed under at Sarcenat. I hope that the bad weather doesn't tire Guiguite too much and doesn't long prevent the vicar's bringing her Holy Communion. Here, the snow came ten days ago Thursday—it fell from 8 o'clock to 4, leaving a blanket of from 5-6 centimeters, a good coat for Hastings. The sun had time to come out for a moment to give all the Sussex landscape an unusual rose glow. Now, everything has melted; but after such a beautiful beginning, we can expect more of the same all through the winter. A few days ago, the weather was still quite mild, and on the cliffs I saw many people snaring little birds, especially bobolinks. I guess the catch is made at the expense of flocks who perch there before crossing the sea. The day before yesterday, we took an all-day walk; it was dry and cold; the woods were covered enchantingly with frost; hardly had I left when I spotted a stream bed with some good rocks containing fossils. My route took me across Battle,[1] so I could take in the market, certainly a beautiful sight. The little town is built along a road which is overrun by cows, and more especially, carts; almost all these carts are russet, attractive and well-kept. The arcade full of buyers—jobbers, robust horse dealers, and slightly contorted farmers with generous beards—showed a series of very noticeable native types; judging by the din coming from the bars, everyone there was in high spirits. Here and there were display cases covered with saucers each containing a small portion of snails soaked in whiskey; judging from the way in which they were being eaten, this must be the traditional delicacy.

Other distractions coming our way included an eclipse of the moon (at midnight, and coinciding with a perfectly clear evening) and the passing of an American squadron on its way to Gravesand. To see it pass, I was on the seashore; the boats were so close to the shore that you could see the shape of their very large masts made of steel grids and looking somewhat like little Eiffel towers. Our Americans didn't hide their joy or their pride. Personally, as I watched this fleet of huge battleships, I had the curious feeling of realizing for the first time that the United States really does exist.

You know as well as we here in England, that about a year from now, there are going to be elections again. For lack of time and maybe even money, it risks being less brilliant; there will be noticeably fewer posters as there were in preceding years. At least you can see how public opinion has developed. The English

1. A small town in Sussex, north of Hastings, so named after the victorious battle (1066) that won William, the Duke of Normandy, the crown of England. See letter 3.

here claim that they can't predict anything. Today we take the oath which Pius X[2] requested. In my capacity as one to be ordained within the year, I must participate in the ceremony: it's the first tangible sign of approaching the priesthood.

My love to you and everyone at Sarcenat; all my prayers.

Pierre

2. The oath against Modernism prescribed by *Motu proprio "Sacrorum antistitum"* of September 9, 1910. See Yves de la Brière, S.J., *"Motu proprio" against Modernism*. Fernand Mourret, in *Revue apologétique,* vol. 35, pp. 601–609, 665–674.

40

My dear Father,

Following the Christmas custom, I'm directing this special letter to you to wish you a happy feast. You know the spirit those away from you join in with those at home (there are quite a few this year). The day after tomorrow, more especially, I will ask God to grant you whatever He deems most desirable for you and the family; this time you realize how close my ordination is, so that next year, a portion of my midnight Masses will be reserved for you.

Once more, it seems that I can give you pleasure only in reassuring you that I always feel more content where I am and where you let me go. To compensate for its undeniable austerity, the theologate has the advantage of ripening many ideas; and I believe that at this time, more than ever, I appreciate the existence God has chosen for me, because I understand the value of this life better—it seems to be going so frighteningly fast!

Let's go on to the local news; most noteworthy is the storm

we had a week ago, the most awful storm I've ever seen. The people in Hastings claim they haven't seen the like since 1874, and what's more, their "parade" was covered with sand and pebbles. At that time, the people barricaded their doors and vents and, at the risk of sleeping poorly, they enjoyed the lovely spectacle. At Ore, we only had wind, but in so special a way that the house trembled. I don't know if there were any mishaps; one thing I do know, the French steamers didn't take on passengers between Friday and Saturday. Finally, today, after a month of bad weather, Sussex reappeared with her hills marvelously clear; emerging from a milky fog, under a lovely, pale, low sun; on days like those, England is truly pretty. If only it could stay as peaceful with its government and traditions; the elections are hardly reassuring, as they brought back a Chamber almost identical to the preceding one. An Englishman told me that the people are really unionists for all practical purposes, but the opinion is swayed by proletarian votes and people who do not see further than a glass of beer.

At Ore, classes stopped yesterday until January 3rd. Now, the end of each school period will bring an ordination. . . . The day after tomorrow I'm going to serve Father Burdo's midnight Mass at his mother's home—the Reparatrix's in Hastings. I suppose, according to tradition, you will be at the Port.[1]

Goodbye, dear Father, my love to you as well as to Mother and everyone at home. Could you please tell Gabriel that I'll write to him next week.

Pierre

1. Notre-Dame-du-Port. See *Letters from Egypt,* letter 19.

Best regards to the rest of the family household, especially Uncle Joseph.

41

Dear Father and Mother,

This is one letter which won't reach you for the 1st of January with the same punctuality as the Christmas note. But since you will be together for a while, that won't cause you any inconvenience. Be assured that from my heart, I wish you the greatest New Year possible, full of everything which could be most agreeable to you, and, above all, the most helpful for you in God's eyes—for He alone remains. I don't have to repeat how much I'm attached to all of you this year. I'm happy to think that finally I will see a few of you. But I'm happier still to think that once I'm a priest I can really intercede for God to bless the whole family. The date of the first ordination seems to be settled now. It will be the 24th (subdiaconate) and February 26th, diaconate (the Sunday before Lent), about a month earlier than anticipated. I'm busy trying to get a breviary; I'm not familiar with

127

it yet. During the triduum for renewal, I'm going to try to get deeper into the mysteries; the triduum takes exceptional place for the Epiphany.

I received Just's note which was lovely, first, because of what it was in itself, and secondly, because of his way of thinking and speaking about Uncle René. Enclosed you will find a word for him and part of a letter my friend Father Robinet sent me from China; he mentions our good Little Mother.

Since my last letter, the days have passed peacefully under the quiet routine of little vacations. My midnight Mass at the Reparatrix convent was very lovely, and afforded me the chance to meet a good number of people staggering in the streets of Hastings, celebrating Christmas. It's quite cold here; the sky is half clear; Wednesday morning, it even snowed a little.

New Year's day brought additional news, Egypt included. My friend, the paleontologist, wrote me after returning from a 32-day expedition on camelback; he was in a place near the Red Sea where it had not rained for seven years. Not long has passed since this made me dream; I will never be totally insensitive to it.

The day before yesterday, a priest from Lisbon came to visit, and since I was out on excursion, I hardly saw him. Among other things, he said that if the search for the king's assassins is not brought to a head, they are threatening to publish some letters which prove that the queen would have wanted to depose her husband, to put her eldest son in his place. I only tell you for what it's worth.

Goodbye, dear Father and Mother; my love to you, to Guiguite and the boys. A special hello to Victor on his feast day. My best to Aunt Marie and Uncle Xavier; I'm not forgetting the children.

Pierre

to Aunt Marie and Uncle Xavier; I'm not forgetting the children.

Pierre

42

Dear Father and Mother,

I'm writing to you rather late, but you will probably realize that it's because of my work, which is more urgent these days. Finally, when I write to you next time, the 15th will have passed, and I will be back in the stream of ordinary work.

To begin, I have to tell you a little disappointment; ordinations[1] scheduled for the 24th and 26th have been scheduled for later on; Mgr. Amigo is booked at St. Matthias for the consecration of a bishop. So, our turn has been put off until later, maybe on the feast of the Annunciation, but nothing has really been decided yet; we just found out about it last night.

Other than the fact that it would be bad manners to ask God for graces faster than He wants to give them, this little delay has the advantage of keeping us from starting the breviary at the beginning of Lent, which is the greatest time for the long,

---

1. From the subdiaconate to the diaconate.

complicated Office—and then, this only makes the priesthood about seven months away.

It made me happy to learn from Mother that Guiguite is finally feeling better; may it last a while this time. Undoubtedly, you must be cold, because for several days here there's been a beautiful sun, an east wind and the temperature hardly goes beyond one degree; at least the weather allows some good football games and agreeable walks. While on one of these walks, I had the chance to meet up with a fox hunt which was well under way; I couldn't see the fox—but the men on horseback crossing a rather bumpy ravine, provided a beautiful sight reminding me of Caran d'Ache's drawings (an inexhaustible source of evenings from yesteryear in Uncle Joseph's living room). I admired the young ladies' steadiness in the saddle more than their dress, and noted the courage of other ladies who were following the chase on foot and via rather dirty trails. It gave me the solemn assurance that in the eyes of the English, I must get spattered in the service of geology.

This week's trips yielded some very beautiful fern prints, but in a rock so huge that I haven't brought it back yet.

Tomorrow, for the feast of the Purification, I'm going to the convent of the Reparatrix Sisters to serve Father Burdo's Mass; he will receive his mother's vows.

To mention something else, vows are coming up here. To honor this, the whole noviciate is coming to Ore. So, it's a solemn day.

Goodbye, dear Father and Mother. My love to you and to Gabriel, Olivier, and Gonzague as well. I pray for you.

Pierre

Last week, Father Vaughan[2] the great preacher (brother of the dead Cardinal) came to give us a talk on his trip to America (for the Eucharistic Congress); since he spoke in English, I didn't understand everything: but just the sight of the speaker was worth it. He gave us a very structured talk. His direction and gestures certainly carry extraordinary power.

2. See C. Martindale, S.J., *Bernard Vaughan, S.J.* (London, 1932).

43

Dear Father and Mother,

About now, you must be starting to find it a long time since my last letter; but you know why. Well, here I am, greatly relieved, having pulled through enough, thanks to Mother's prayers; from now well into the future, I don't foresee any extra or special work coming to spice up the ordinary run-of-the-mill day. It's an advantage and disadvantage all at once, for rarely has time seemed to go so quickly as it has during the past month.

May I tell you, first of all, that ordination day has been set once more. It will be the 25th and 26th of March. So, the delay isn't that great; I even noticed that the subdiaconate coincides with the anniversary of my vows. To answer Father's question, St. Matthias isn't a special feast in England; but the feasts of the apostles are among the days set aside for episcopal consecrations; in the present case, this involves the coadjutor of Mgr. Burnes, archbishop of Westminster.

Since my last letter, and up until now, when a westerly storm has been raging, the weather has been marvelous, hardly cold at all. Uncle Joseph could almost come to spend the winter here. Despite everything, and due to the water, maybe, the grass isn't getting green yet.

As I told you, I accompanied Father Burdo when his mother took the habit; the ceremony was very moving, all the more since everything took place in calmness and simplicity. For the canonical questioning, Father Burdo said, "My Daughter . . .," and she answered, "My Father . . ." I don't know if the new religious will stay here long enough for Mother to see her in August.

Last Sunday, Mr. Dawson, my geologist friend, paid me a visit. In regard to our offer to send the British Museum our last fern (imprinted in a block of about 12 kilograms) he said he would take the responsibility of carrying it, and left here carrying it under his arm, with vigor at that. I think the sample is more beautiful than the species is rare; but that will at least give us an exact appraisal.

Thank you for sending me Françoise's letter; a letter we have here from China mentions a beautiful profession and clothing ceremony at the Little Sisters' in Shanghai. Françoise must have really done honor to the house for the event.[1]

1. With her usual humor, Françoise wrote to her sister, Guite: "Mgr. Paris officiated, and Mother would have enjoyed seeing the choir filled with Jesuit Fathers, among whom were such distinguished personalities as the Superior of Shang-Nan (Father Gilot, who very well remembers how he questioned little Albéric in Jersey), the Rector of Zi-ka-wei, and the famous Father Froc who loves the Little Sisters of the Poor almost as much as he loves typhoons. I was on pins and needles. Fortunately, my assistant was the former Rev. Mother of our House; she is always my life-saver on occasions like those." (Letter of February 5, 1911.) Father Louis Froc (Brest, 1859—Paris, 1932) nicknamed "Father of ty-

Goodbye, dear Father and Mother; my love to you and all at home. I pray for you.

Pierre

---

phoons," directed the observatory at Zi-ka-wei and made great contributions to the field of navigation. When he died, expressions of grief and esteem came from all over the world. See Henri Gauthier in *Etudes,* vol. 213 (1932), pp. 273-286. The works are cited in the periodical *Archivum hist. S.J.,* III, 241; IV, 205-207.

44

Dear Father and Mother,

This letter is being written on a beautiful day which happily ends a long spell of rain and squalls. Spring isn't here yet; it's later than ever in coming, but it's obviously just around the corner. If only this good weather could extend to you, and help Marguerite get on her feet—at least may God take the care of soothing her when He Himself deems acceptable.

As in all the years past, I repeat again that I'll be thinking of you especially on the 7th, for Albéric's anniversary; although it's impossible for us not to feel it, don't we have to think that it's really a day to celebrate, because his was a beautiful life to the very end, and doubtlessly such as God expected of him. I'll be so happy six months from now, when I'll be able to say Mass for such occasions.

At Ore Place, there's nothing really new understandably; as

austere as it seems, Lent announces the coming of Easter. Lent is going to be a bit broken up in three weeks by the ordinations; it's also the time when fourth-year scholastics stop going to classes in order to prepare for the final exam—that will be my lot in a year's time, and interested parties will meet it with a certain pride. Added to that, we're building a little wing onto the house; it's going to give building *aficianados* (I'm not among them) the joy of seeing the workers; by this, you can judge that our present days are not absolutely bereft of amusements.

The catalogue of Jersey minerals I laboriously put together two years ago is finally going to appear in the *Annales de la Société Jersiaise,* which isn't very famous, but at least it will establish somewhere the results of all those walks while in philosophy.[1] The first proofs were horrible; the most amusing—though not the worst—typographical error had me speak of "*filous* (read *filons*[2]) injected into the diorite."

You will probably have learned through the Montlaurs or others that in Cannes, little Father de Moré was very ill with an infectious grippe; he was resting there during the winter; they even gave him the last rites. Right now, he seems to have pulled out of it, but is far from being well.

Think of it! we've been following the reorganization of the ministry with great interest; but God really has ways of pulling us through things or drawing good out of evil.

Right now, we're reading *The Pope and the Council* (of Basel) by Noël Valois, which is a very big book, unfortunately, but

1. See *Bibliographie C. Cuénot,* I, no. 7. The publication of the *Société Jersiaise, bulletin annuel* in 1910, was probably behind schedule.
2. A play on words; *filou* means pickpocket, *filon* means vein. —Tr.

which is giving us a chance to know the Church of the twentieth century.[3]

I must close now. My love to all of you.

Pierre

3. *Le pape et le concile (1418–1450)*, 2 vols. (Paris, 1909).

45

Dear Father and Mother,

In writing to you tonight, I can't forget that it was twelve years ago to the hour that we parted; it's all the more the day to re-assure you of my affection for, in a week's time, I shall have benefited from the happiest consequences of the sacrifice you made then. You can count that on Saturday, and Sunday, my prayers will be filled with you. I can tell you that I see Orders coming up with more joy than I could ever have imagined. Now I desire them with conviction because I sense the need to be ful-filled and to work for God with the greatest possible efficacy. He will listen to you if, after having given me to Him, you ask Him to prepare me on the 25th and 26th to be a true priest. Through vows, a person really has the feeling of giving himself; through Orders, a person has to feel especially accepted.

The ceremony will be very simple: Wednesday night, we will begin a triduum, then ordinations will take place Saturday and Sunday. I'll drop you a note at the beginning of next week.

The last two weeks have been spent in the calm of Lent; the new building is rising little by little, to the great joy of enthusiasts; one after the other, the seniors are finishing their classes. I've had new contacts with the British Museum over an iguanodon footprint recently discovered in the cliffs; it's of special interest, as it distinctly reveals the animal's skin wrinkles—it lends a real-life quality to the piece. Judging from a photograph, the Museum deemed the specimen desirable; unfortunately, since the print is 30 to 40 centimeters long, and since the block is hardly accessible, I doubt that it can be lifted out before the sea has completely deteriorated it.

Incidentally, I learned that Wednesday night, my famous little mammiferous molar is to be presented to the London Geographical Society.

In the papers, you will have read about the attempt to rob Abbé Loiseau in Paris: I know him well, and he has often put me up there. Fortunately, he wasn't badly hurt.

Goodbye, dear Father and Mother. My love to you as well as to Guiguite and your big boys.

Pierre

46

Dear Father and Mother,

The second ordination is over; I'm a deacon. And as I told you in my last letter, I'm also completely happy, especially in the conviction that I've begun to become a better instrument for God; may He use me for a lot of good.

Evidently, a person senses that being a deacon still isn't everything; having taken 2 steps creates a great desire to make the third. But you have to know how to wait patiently and to earn it. Five months is not so long, and in five months, at the end of a very similar feast, you will find that I've already said Mass twice.

So, thank God with me. Yesterday and today, I didn't neglect to pray for the family, as I consider myself a bit as its representative before the Lord. Causing me to pray more effectively and often, the breviary will also help me to think about it still more regularly. Did you notice that I was ordained subdeacon ten years to the day, after my vows? I like to see it as a sign of Our Lady of the Port's protection; then too, I was happy to have the Blessed Virgin's office as the first to recite.

Thank you for your letters during the week, and thanks also to Gabriel and Guiguite for theirs. As you say, Joseph's lot seems to be all right in the end, which was the most desirable. If he really wishes, he can get something useful out of it even from his two years, at least to strengthen himself.

I'm writing during bad enough weather; after two rather-warm days, sudden showers came down from the North yesterday, and this morning, we woke to find a heavy coat of snow. Maybe this cold hasn't reached you.

I find M. de Bretenières' desire to bring back the martyr's[1] body a bit strange; if I were in the latter's shoes, I'd rather see my remains staying in Korea without even considering the fact that doubtlessly, it would be better prayed for over there.

I must stop now.

My love and prayers to you.

Pierre

---

1. See M. d'Hulst, *Vie de Just de Bretenières, missionnaire apostolique martyrisé en Corée en 1866,* 2nd edition (Paris, 1892). See letter 24 above.

47

Dear Father and Mother,

Our vacation finished yesterday, and the last trimester has begun; we aren't far from the end. For the past two weeks the weather has been almost constantly beautiful, and since conditions there must be the same, Murol must be fully into its Spring glory; but the fact that Guiguite can't enjoy it must diminish a lot of its enchantment. Don't you think that when the first opportunity arises, even if it means risking a little, it would be good to go to Lourdes? I realize it entails a very delicate decision; nevertheless, if an occasion presents itself, it would be a shame to miss it.

I had your news through M. de Gurgy;[1] he belongs to the Canterbury house, but came here for a few days along with many other priests on their way back from Lenten assignments, as he himself was. Everyone is more or less enthused over the first

1. Father Joseph de Gurgy (1876–1956) was the bursar for the Jesuit Province of Lyons for a long time.

try; it's quite understandable since they realized for the first time in a tangible way, the utility of things they had been made to do for so many years. Among the priests was Father Poidebard[2] who is going back to Armenia in August.

With beautiful days, the countryside is growing prettier; the meadows are filled with very frisky lambs, and the underbrush is carpeted with wildflowers, while waiting for the hyacinths. During the week, some swallows and cuckoos came, and, in the cliffs, I even found a viper, but I couldn't capture it. In the heronry at Brede, the herons are busy building nests; in a couple of weeks, I have to bring an American priest-ornithologist there, and thanks to his patronage, I suppose, I can observe the population from closer up.

For the time being, I haven't been able to find him a green woodpecker.

Tell Joseph that I received the letter he wrote before leaving Angers. I think that if I had been at Puy, as he was, I wouldn't have been able to resist the desire to go collecting sapphires in the stream at Expailly.

Goodbye, dear Father and Mother. My love to you and your big ones.

Pierre

2. Father Antoine Poidebard, pioneer in archaeological research by airplane (1878–1955). See *Grand Larousse encycl.*, vol. 8. In *L'Histoire et ses méthodes*, Collectif Samaran (Paris, 1961) the study: *Méthodes modernes de l'archéologie*, by R. Bloch. The magazine *Archivum hist.*, S.J., XXIV, 388, 389; XXV, 706, 707.

48

Dear Father and Mother,

   With the date of this letter in mind, I can only think that in 3 months to this very day, I will see you here on the eve of my ordination. Sunday I won't neglect praying Our Lady of the Port to prepare me for this day—as much for my sake as for yours, since it bears upon the growth of the family that I make a good priest.[1] In compliance with Mother's request, I shall keep

1. Françoise wrote to her mother from China on May 1st: "How happy you will be on August 26th. In case my next letter doesn't arrive on time, please tell Pierre how much I will be united to him on that very beautiful day; because of the Manchurian plague, I don't know if my annual letter reached him. Anyway, please ask him to remember me as well as our house in China in a special way at his first Mass; tell him to thank God with me and for me. May He grant me the only grace and happiness in this world, to live and die in this dear mission which I love so deeply. The thought of many separations must come to you, no doubt, but think, dear Mother, that it is one of your own children who is carrying all your sacrifices directly to God and who intercedes for all those away from you. Do not rue the China which separates us and, believe on the contrary, that

145

a room for you, and I even think that you will have one where the people speak a little French.

We are deep in Spring here, and only the ash trees are still almost black; for the past two weeks it has hardly rained. Only last week, while you were having storms, here it was gray for a few days with very cold winds coming from the north.

To come to something interesting for Biel, the block from Bayssat does not seem to be a meteorite, unfortunately. After looking at the samples, the Museum told me that the rock is a basalt, of a variety common in Auvergne in general and in Limagne in particular. Also, the whitened surface indicates a slow alteration and not a fusion, which surely would have produced a black enamel. So it must be admitted that the stone had been in the field for a very long time; it's one of those curious instances where internal criteria, as they say, supplant the seemingly best-established likelihoods. For Gabriel, there remains the consolation of having done his duty under the circumstance; some other time, he'll be better rewarded.

Last Thursday, I went back to the heronry, escorting my American friend (who went back to Missouri yesterday), armed with good field glasses.

---

you can't unite anything better to your Jesuit's first Mass . . . In God, my dear Mother, we will be reunited, you know where, and the sacrifice which separates us on earth will reunite us up there."

That was her last letter; on the night of May 27th, seized by a fit of vomiting, she was obliged to go to bed; she had been hit by smallpox. During her eleven days of heroic sufferings, she confided some messages to a religious: "I will pray for Papa . . . Tell Mother that I die happily and without regret, since I die a Little Sister of the Poor in China. Don't let her grieve too much. I remain their child, grateful for everything they have done for me. I shall pray for Guite and my brothers. May Pierre pray for me; in heaven I shan't forget him." Assisted by Father Froc, she died on June 7th.

While going through Brede, I went to its church for the first time; like most country churches in the area, it's the old Catholic pre-Reformation style, gothic with a square tower. As its pastor is a ritualist, the interior is very stylish, even a bit of a museum. There are old keys—ancient bell clappers—and the bed (!) of a ferocious giant, sort of the local Bluebeard; to get this bed in, it had to be sawed in two—and above all, Swift's own cradle. The herons were at their stations, crying like geese, and very busy with their young who seemed almost big enough to fly. With binoculars, we could follow all their movements, the most original was to see them feeding their young. The little herons flapped their wings, stretched out their necks as their parents shoved their beaks down astounding depths, moving like a machine piston. Perched immobile on the tops of the oaks, claws open, wings outstretched, the whole flock of big birds presented a curious spectacle which even enthused my American friend. A peasant told us that the heronry was in another woods a few years ago, but the owner cut down the trees; that displeased the birds, so they moved elsewhere.

The day we went, there were numerous nightingales in the woods; they can't really like the immediate seaside, for Ore never hears them.

Goodbye, dear Father and Mother; my love to you and to all at home. Thank Gabriel for his last letter.

Pierre

49

Dear Father and Mother,

This morning, directly from Shanghai (via one of our Fathers,[1] I think) came the telegram announcing that Françoise had just gone to join Albéric. You offered God your dear daughter: so now, He has accepted her for good. He alone is the end of all things, so that when He takes someone to Himself, it isn't to separate, but to unite. May His will be done. I know you will have repeated this often, for three days, without its having prevented you from suffering cruelly; I would give so much to be with you at this time, and to be able to speak to you a little. Isn't our consolation the fact that it's hard to dream of a holier and more beautiful end? Françoise truly found the death she desired above all things, —she reiterated this in her last letter— in China and for China. Without a doubt it was a joy to us to know that she could talk to us from further and further away; —and aren't we a bit selfish crying so much as we see her

1. Father Froc. See Letter 43.

already at the end she had desired as a distant ideal, and for which she tired herself every day of her life?

How many times she told me of her desire to go to see God as soon as possible . . .

Our Lord rewarded her before time: we don't even have the right to regret that she would have done more good had she lived longer. The beautiful life is that which fulfills God's plans. In Françoise you formed and gave God a saint: you could not have dreamed of a better future for your child.

—Here they will pray much for her and for you; I also sent word to Canterbury where the Mass intentions will be numerous. But I really believe that few prayers will touch God as will those of the aged whom Françoise sent to Paradise, especially the Chinese.

Courage, my poor Father and Mother; the moments of suffering pass, and they will go to God: it's then that a person can offer something to God and earn something which allows him to appear before God with confidence. Know that your remaining children love you even more, and would give anything to comfort you.

My love to you, Gabriel, Yéyé and Gonzague. A special remembrance for our poor Guiguite.

Pierre

50

Dear Father and Mother,

The reason for this letter is to let Mother know that the stipend for her Masses came, and that the Masses themselves started being said yesterday, the 16th. But besides, I'm happy to see the opportunity to keep more in contact at this time. Like yourselves, I'm anxious to get details from Shanghai; I think the Fathers over there will send particulars, and naturally, I shall send them on to you. The day before yesterday, the Mission's bursar, M. Tournade, came by (he's from Auvergne, as you know, and head chaplain of the Catholic Youth movement, —in parenthesis, he's undoubtedly going to Etang for a stay before long); he was cut to the quick over the loss of our Little Sister as they were counting a lot on her, and he promised his prayers. This year, Kiang-Nan is going through a real crisis; be it because of the famine or for others reasons, 12 missionaries have died in 10 months, six (of the 12) were district superiors; and the

bad season has only just begun. From Canterbury, Father Poidebard and Father de Gurgy asked me to let you know that they
share your sorrow and promise you their prayers. I continue to
think of you; the first moments of sorrow are not the ones in
which a person is most aware of the loss; but with time, and
God's help, a person comes to a better understanding of a trial's
providential side. And especially in Françoise's case, the more a
person thinks about her life, the more he discovers that God gave
her one more exquisitely beautiful than she could have dared to
wish.

Here are some little bits of news from Ore. Tonight begins a
Renewal triduum which ends on the 21st. Also, classes end definitively on that day—reviewing for exams begins. Undoubtedly
we are going to celebrate the feast of St-Louis de G. with the
novices at St. Leonard's. Then, the next day is a big day for the
whole of England; actually, the big question is this: "Will it
rain for the Coronation?" It must be said that the drought continued to be absolute until this evening when short but heavy
torrents fell. For the festivities, let's hope that the good weather
keeps up until Thursday or Friday; the farmers do need rain:
the hayfields are miserable and, in certain places in the North,
the lambs are dying because their mothers cannot feed them.

Finally, I received a copy of the London Geographical Society's
journal (May) which has the description and drawing of my
famous mammiferous tooth; unfortunately, I only have one tear
sheet, —otherwise, I would have sent you a copy.

It will interest Father to know that for the past few days in the
woods, close by, I have seen several bifolium orchids and a
colony of *orphis apifera.*

Goodbye, dear Father and Mother; my love to you and those who are at Sarcenat; I think about you often.

Pierre

Here's what Françoise said to me in her last letter: "Don't forget that I'm holding you to your promise to ask Our Lord at your first Mass that He deign to take me to Him completely and that He keep me in China until I die."

51

Dear Father,

I have just written Mother for her birthday, but I can't help adding a word for you, if only to tell you once more that I'm very united to you during these days when Françoise must be on your mind more intensely. Since my last letter, news from Shanghai came, and despite all the comforting things, I'm afraid they will still bring you their sadness: they bring back many memories; they make the fact of separation living and concrete; and then, when you read them, you realize how powerless words are to express what could have been captured in a look, a moment of conversation or a remembered word. Ten letters would not suffice, and besides, we can hardly count on any more after what we've received. It's the ransom of China and this separation that have won Françoise an end the likes of which she hardly dared hope. At least we know that she was happy when she died; she went where her desires carried her. Isn't that the essential thing? The fact remains that God asked you for a very hard sacrifice, my poor Father, which has sense only for those who believe in Our Lord crucified, the value of suffering, and in the extreme disproportion between the pains and joys of the present, and those which await us.

Yesterday, I received a letter of condolence from the Assistant Mother Superior in Shanghai. She didn't add anything new to what you already know, except that they have no idea where and when Françoise could have contracted the disease, and also, that no one else in the house has had it.

To return to the little chronicle of Ore Place, we're in the midst of sitting for final exams, which is quite a strain, especially at our age. As for Coronation Day, I only saw Hastings' streets adequately decked out with the loud tricolor. It was worse here than in London, and we couldn't take part on the 22nd because of the rain and the wind. On the night of the 23rd, with just a little rain, we lit up Ore Place with different things which delighted us and proved a real source of great amusement. Even the trails of fog brushing the house were a big help, tinting everything with the colors from our Bengali flares. There were no casualties, which made us happier than they were at the English scholasticate (near Lancashire) where a Father blew up his hand with some fireworks. It's amazing to see with what togetherness and spontaneity the English feasted their king, at the same time that half of them seem to be working to destroy the regime. Is their conduct contradictory, or must a person admit that England can keep its tradition and remain united while renewing its constitutions?

Today, interest is focused on airplanes which leave Calais tomorrow at dawn for Brighton; if they follow the sea (which makes the trip a bit longer, but safer) we won't miss seeing them from here. Would you believe that I knew the Master of Novices in Jersey? I scarcely remember him. Goodbye, my dear Father; my love to you as well as to Biel and Yéyé. A special hello to Gonzague: I'll be thinking about him on the 5th. Thursday I thought of Yéyé when I saw a beautiful pike in the Brede; an American told me that, back home, they use a mouse to bait this kind of fish!

Pierre

52

My dear Mother,

The chalice came yesterday, safe and sound; thank you for having chosen such a beautiful one. It will seem even better in less than three months . . .

Thank you for your last letter; tell Guig. and Gabriel that their letters gave me great pleasure. Here, everything is going as well as usual. I'll write you at greater length at the end of the week. My love to you.

Pierre

53

Dear Father and Mother,

Enclosed is a list of the best trains to take for Hastings. If you aren't afraid of being travel-fatigued, the most convenient train is the one that gets you into Hastings at 4:44 p.m., via Folkestone. If you arrive on the 23rd at that hour, you will have time to stop at the hotel, then take a tram which will get you into Ore at 6 P.M. (we're having a reception on the 23rd from 6 to 6:30). No doubt, a Father from Folkestone will meet the train and give the needed information. If you prefer to arrive on the 22nd, let me know the exact time you'll be getting off at Hastings; someone from the boarding house will be there to meet you (also on the 23rd). Rooms with twin beds are hard to find in England. Just the same, I did hold a pretty one overlooking the sea, where you can pull yourselves together: the others were smaller and not as good. The trip to England isn't hard; if you go through Dover, don't take the train which stops at the dock, as that one goes to London; go instead to the town station. If you go through Folkestone, rest assured that your train stops at Ashford. Ashford is a complex little station where you have to change trains in all eventuality; you always have a long wait there. You can change French money on the steamer. Don't be afraid to bring warm clothing; if the weather spoils two weeks from now, which is likely, you could feel quite chilly. If you need new information, write to me, even during retreat (from the 16th to the 24th).

It seems funny to be sending you all these details, and it's hard to realize that we'll be seeing each other in a few days when I am a priest. Pray for me between now and then. It continues to be very warm and dry here. The last heat wave was the day before yesterday; it hit 30°, an unheard-of record.

My week was active enough: it began with a trip to Wadhurst, a little old-fashioned English town located on one of the three main cirques in the hills surrounding Hastings (they extend from Folkestone to Eastbourne, touching Tamise to the north). The country there is beautiful, quite rolling and generously wooded. The big parks are numerous and the architecture of the manors is less severe than is customary; I had to cross through one of them which had no deer, but to make up for it, there were hundreds of half-wild ducks on the pond, and some geese, I think.

Monday, thanks to a remarkably cheap tourist train, I went on as far as Selsey, a peninsula located across from Wight's eastern coast, in the hopes of finding some interesting rock banks; this hope was partly disappointed, but at least the trip itself was interesting.

Selsey is a large strip of flat land with huge fields of red clover, and then, as it comes close to the sea, there are pastures. In

Saxon days, this corner of the country was an important center, with its own bishopric, but the region was ruined when the coast eroded. The bishop's old deer park is under water and the golf course that replaces it is marked "the Park" on the map. Chichester has replaced Selsey. The coast is very low, naturally, but the sea is less muddy and more rich in algae than it is at Hastings—on the day I was there, it was hard to distinguish Wight. I spent one or two hours in Chichester, which suffices when one is not an archaeologist. The town is very small and dead, built at four great crossroads which were important ancient Roman routes. The cathedral is especially worth seeing; it is hardly bigger than Notre Dame du Port, has a Romanesque nave, gothic aisles, a long choir and an isolated bell tower; it dates from the eleventh century and must stir up a world of memories for anyone sufficiently versed in history. Grafted to one side of the church is a square cloister with pointed arches made of oak beams with finely carved arcades circling a very poetic, medieval churchyard. I went in during evening services; without measuring up to the Offices in Canterbury, the music was still religious and very beautiful, and I stayed to listen for a long time; the atmosphere was impressive.

The return to Hastings had its particular charm. From the train there's a good view of Arundel; an oblique ray of sun made the many turrets stand out. After Brighton, when we crossed the South Downs whose curved sides are a bit reminiscent of peaks, there were trails of fog and a full moon, which gave a very pretty effect.

I didn't tell you that ten days ago, the young students visited us from Canterbury, and on that occasion, I met three little Chinese; I was very moved when one came over to me to talk about Françoise, and to convey the greeting she had given him for me a year ago. Preparing for your arrival here, I forgot to tell you something about the trams. They leave from a little spot near the sea called Memorial (after the memorial statue of Prince Albert, located at the center and marked by the presence of a clock). To get to Ore Place, you have to take the tram marked "Circular" or "St. Helens" but not "Ore," and ask for a ticket for St. Helens (3 pence); the trip lasts a good half hour and you get off near the big cemetery. From there, you're only a few minutes from Ore Place; it's enough to back-track fifty metres and take the first descending road to the right. At Memorial, you take the trams which run perpendicular to the sea.

And now, goodbye, dear Father and Mother. My special love to Guiguite and Yéyé; my prayers for all of you.

Pierre

54

Dear Father and Mother,

Here it is almost two weeks already since we said the goodbye
which ended your stay to witness the ordination; it seemed like
an interminably long time before ordination day arrived.[1] So
pass all things, the best as the saddest. Happy are we to whom
God grants the potential to hold onto them a bit forever, and
to know the part we did for Him in all those things. Under
the circumstances, I really believe that this part was so primary
that I can still feel the effect of those happy days in August; they
will have made us love each other more, and Our Lord, too.
What's more, every time I think about it, I regret not having
known sufficiently how to express the great affection I felt for
you, especially so soon after our Françoise's death. Just the same,
you knew what I meant.

1. Ordination to the priesthood had been conferred on Pierre and his
classmates on August 24th, by Bishop Amigo. He said his first Mass on
the 25th: Pierre was assisted by Father Joseph Roullet, prefect of the college in Cairo; the Mass was served by his two brothers, Gabriel and
Joseph. Victor and Gonzague were with their parents.

About the intervention of Bishop Amigo on the death of Tyrrell in 1907:
see Blondel and Valensin, *Correspondance,* vol. I, p. 371; vol. 2, pp. 75–88.

Since the memorable day when we separated on the dock at Ore, my life has been extremely calm, quite transformed by morning Mass, and the knowledge that I am finally a priest. The beautiful weather hasn't let up; on the 8th there was a heat wave comparable to the one in August; the meadows which had begun to be green, returned to gray. Nonetheless, the sun slants, and the days are getting shorter quickly.

Once more, oil tankers glide on the sea which has become like a mirror. I can't look at them without thinking about the boys. Since you left, I haven't seen the Memorial, nor Oxo, nor Mrs. Cameron's roof. On the contrary, I've gone back to exploring the cliffs, and Saturday, I even went to Ashford to say a Mass on the following Sunday. The Catholic church is right on the edge of the city, where the fields begin; the adjoining rectory is small, but comfortable, tidy, with many knickknacks, notably a display of cats (made of porcelain, cloth or plush), more or less mis-shapen or sardonic, a real nightmare to behold. I noticed a match box depicting the back view of 2 black cats, a big one with a huge arched back, and a little one with a smooth back, bearing the warning, "Don't scratch me; scratch my mother." As for Ashford, it seemed dull and dingy; seen from the station—the rectory was pretty—the rest, loads of red houses lost in lots of greenery. The Catholic congregation isn't that large, but very united; the curate himself is excellent and very intelligent. I spent a large part of the morning reading *Christ in the Church,* Benson's last work, it was extraordinarily pleasing.[2] In the evening, before going back to Hastings, I went to see two of the

2. Pierre Teilhard was an avid reader of Benson, even though he was critical of some of his ideas. See *Ecrits du temps de la guerre* (1965), pp. 87–88.

numerous estates neighboring Ashford (all rented out by their short-of-cash owners); one of them has a secluded place where England's poet laureat (I've forgotten his name) lives in quite an original old house. You are familiar with this type of place: meadows sewn irregularly with magnificent trees; at Ashford, young elms are dominant.

At the end of the month (from the 26th to the 30th) I'm decidedly going to give a retreat at Malvern, located on the southern border near Wales; I'll say more about them later.

Enclosed is a postcard of the church at Hastings; it's the card Father wanted to buy for Mother the last day you were here.

For ordination, I received a note from Father Froc, dated the feast of St. Frances de Chantal.

My love to you as well as to Guiguite and the boys; my prayers are for you every morning. I'll get around to writing the boys; they're probably very busy now.

Pierre

55

Dear Father and Mother,

This is the night before I leave for Malvern (near Worcester) where I'm going for four or five days to preach to a group of adult boarders at the convent of some exiled religious. Even though there's nothing to fear, still and all, this first try makes me somewhat apprehensive. I'm quite anxious to get going. Let's hope that Our Lord will let me do some good. In itself, and if I had the time or desire to see the countryside, the trip is interesting; I go through Oxford; Malvern, so they say, is very lovely, backed as it is by the first mountains in Wales. Tomorrow morning, I'm going to see London again, which will remind me of last month. It's exactly a month since I said my first Mass.

These days, I'll keep all of you, and Albéric especially, in mind; even though there's hardly a need, it would make me happy to say a Mass for him; and I believe that my prime intention will be to thank God for giving him such a beautiful and good life, albeit very short. Unfortunately, it is impossible for me to say this Mass on the 27th, as it is already set aside (for thanksgiving and in memory of the founding of the Society); the Mass for Albéric will be on the 26th.

For the last ten days or so, the weather has grown colder here, but there has been relatively little rain yet. We are into a beautiful ordinary autumn, and the countryside is greener than it was in August. I have noticed that during the past two months, the Hastings Museum has been enriched by a beautiful collection of local birds—which stirred up regrets that I hadn't brought Father there. Above all, there are lots of ducks and water fowl (Eider ducks, red crested birds [netta rufina]), almost all killed off in the past few years. Leaving the museum, I saw a part-albino sparrow.

The turnover of scholastics at Ore has brought many new faces, foreign for the most part. This time, we have some Portuguese, and two from Mozambique; but none took part in the revolution.

A short time ago, the clay cliffs disclosed a very lovely new kind of cone. I'm still looking for a paleobotanist.

From another perspective, the bushy sections of the cliffs are inhabited by many pheasants who fly off in a formation which makes a tempting target.

Goodbye for now, dear parents; my love to you as well as to the boys; I think of all of you each morning.

Pierre

56

Ore Place
October 8, 1911

Dear Father and Mother,

Due to my trip to Malvern, breaking up my schedule in a novel way, I have a feeling that I haven't written to you in weeks; yet my letter is dated only two weeks ago. At the present time, we have "returned," if this word can have any meaning to those who hardly go out, —stated otherwise, classes have resumed; despite the fact that we're still getting off the ground, the year can be said to be under way. For me, it means only five or six more months of classes; the end will come quickly; mine is a privileged situation. I came back from my first "apostolic trip" as content as possible. The subject was easy—maybe less inspiring than was hoped; but I discovered that it is easy to talk about my convictions to people who really want to know, and more, I felt the power the priesthood gives to counsel, to console and to come closer to God. Also, my impression last Sunday, as I finished my last sermon, was quite different from the relief a person feels on completing some drudgery. Also, without its really disquieting me, I'll be seeing myself in quite some other kind of ministry.

The secular aspect of the trip was much more interesting and filled with the unexpected; here are some glimpses. I left on the same train which took us to London in August; the best stop was in South Kensington; then, around 1:30, from Paddington, a luxurious "Great Western Railway" express took me non-stop to Worcester. The railway goes through rolling countryside comparable to a series of concentric washbowls, the bottom being London. The edges of these bowls usually have beautiful parks; especially outside Reading, the country becomes wild in parts, with a few houses made of gray stone which camouflages them.

In Worcester, I hardly saw anything except the cathedral's square tower; half an hour afterward, I got off at Malvern, located in a certainly beautiful corner. If it weren't for the granite rocks, a person could believe himself carried off before a string of mountain peaks: in the middle of a plain where the Severn and Avon Rivers flow, a chain of green hills rises abruptly to about 500 meters, running from north to south for a good twenty kilometers. Malvern lies about half way, and the Crosier Sisters' convent clings to the slope quite a way up. That is where I stayed for five days, prey to the solicitude of a good Breton extern Sister whose aim was to stuff me with good food. Thanks to my sturdy legs, I could use my free time to explore the countryside at leisure; it is quite captivating. The main town is a fashionable, elegant resort; many beautiful villas tucked in among shrubs and covered with climbing vines. In the center is an old priory founded by a Saxon monk; the architecture is Norman, one of those rare English churches, it seems, whose stained-glass windows were not shattered during the Reformation; unfortunately, many of the windows are incoherent as it was formerly customary to replace broken pieces with fragments taken from windows which couldn't be seen as well; nevertheless, there is a series of scenes from Genesis. They are deliciously naïve. Due to its geographical position, Malvern has always been an important center. On one of the peaks remain accentuated vestiges of a Breton camp where Caractacus must have held out with his Silurians during the Roman campaigns. During the Middle Ages, this was a land of great forests and magnificent hunts. Many kings called it theirs. For those knowing their English history well, there must be enough substance for long reminiscences high in the Malvern Hills.

I climbed them several times, for the view is just gorgeous: to the east is Worcester plain and Glocestershire; to the west, Hereford's plain going as far as Monmouth, Shropshire and the Welsh mountains, which aren't too majestic but venerable nonetheless. Then, in the larch-laced pastures are sheep with black hoofs and muzzles, so often seen on the English hillsides. You know that I couldn't go near the Silurian shales (granite rises from the middle) without collecting some trilobites which I found by myself the very first time! Last Monday, I really had to go back to Ore. This time I stopped in Oxford for a day, thanks to the generous hospitality of our English Fathers who are the curates of the Catholic church there. Once again, I regretted that I didn't know my English history better. I might have been able to stir up some reminiscences stored in the old gothic colleges with their gray wrought-iron works standing out against well-clipped, strikingly-green lawns. The Bodléienne Library was closed; but for the students' trunks, golf clubs and tennis raquets, there was plenty of space to move around, and I took advantage

168

PIERRE TEILHARD DE CHARDIN

of it. St. Mary's was especially attractive to me because of its memories of Cranmer and Newman,[1] and Christ-Church College, in particular, filled me with admiration. Maybe Father remembers the gigantic gothic refectory serviced by a Gargantuan kitchen and dominated by a classic tableau of Henry VIII who used to give banquets there. I was deeply impressed by English traditionalism, not so much by particular monuments as by the total town, with its profusion of ancient houses, —its streets, where apart from cars in particular, you only see "handsomes"[2] and horse-drawn carriages, —its shaded parks which make a belt along the river.

Tuesday morning, I left Oxford and once again spent some time in London, reaching Charing Cross at the same time as the negro Johnson[3] in person, who was flanked by an obsequious trainer, just as black, dressed just as brightly from head to foot, and equally as colossal. Perhaps most curious was to see how everyone's attention was turned towards them, just as though the objects of attention were curious animals.

All these little things rarely distracted me from things more important in themselves, like the war in Tripoli. I was shaken by the *Liberté's* disaster, —all the more when I read in the English paper that M. Joubert was in command.

My love to you both, dear parents. Thank Guiguite for her last letter and Françoise's picture. I pray for you all every morning.

Pierre

1. On Teilhard and Newman, see Blondel and Teilhard, *Mémoires échangés en décembre 1919* (Bibliothèque des Archives de philosophie, new series, vol. I, 1966).
2. Hansoms. —Tr.
3. A famous boxer at that time.

169

57

Dear Father and Mother,

As you have probably guessed, I thought especially of the family last week—of its deceased and its saints. In saying Mass on the 1st, each time I called upon those in Paradise, I thought I was undoubtedly calling on Françoise and all the others. On the 2nd, my Mass was for all our dead; it was just the anniversary of Loulou's birth. All this should make us think about heaven so that we have more heart to fill our lives well.

These past two weeks have been spent in studies and in peace. There were a few nice days here and there, but the stormy weather still remains; today in particular, we are going through a violent wind storm from the west. It kills the poetry of the land; the leaves are going as soon as they turn yellow; it's feared that in a few days Ashburnham will have lost all its autumn splendor. Speaking of woods, a game keeper recently told us some rather curious things about pheasant hunting. On the estate he guards (near Battle, on the right as you come from Hastings) they don't start shooting until Christmas day so that the birds are fatter, but then, it's a slaughter. The hunters follow the paths the pheasants are used to taking to find their food, and at the end of the day, you can count a good hundred dead ones. It doesn't seem too attractive. Meantime, the warden's teeth are on edge because poachers come in the night to hit the perched and sleeping pheasants with slingshots. The warden's job is made easier by the noise the disturbed birds make when they fly away. I finally found out where to have my plant fossils analyzed; a paleobotanist from Cambridge, who has already done a book on imprints found around Hastings, wants to see them. I'm preparing them now to send to him. It's the beginning of the dispersion for what I have collected here in three years; among the plants, those which are worthwhile will undoubtedly go directly from Cambridge to South-Kensington. It's the nicest thing that could happen to them.

I'm happy that Gonzague took his failure well and I congratulate him. Tell him that I wish him a belated happy birthday (and P. Lenoir[1] as well) and that I'll write to him without too much delay. Good hunting! I thought of the tradition while reading *millia signati;* but I don't think it would be worth it in England. On the first, there were still a few migrating swallows around Ore.

In the cliffs east of Hastings, bird catchers stretch out their nets in abundance to catch the unfortunate yellow-hammers and other little birds about to cross the water no doubt. It's pitiful.

My love to you both and to all at home.

Pierre

1. See *Letters from Egypt,* letter 51.

58

Dear Father and Mother,

These past two weeks have gone by in almost absolute tranquillity, and the marked absence of anything eventful. The sun is beginning to stay low on the horizon, and the trees have become almost all black; it's the end of Autumn, and a bad Autumn at that. Up until today, when the north wind brought cold, blue skies, we have hardly emerged from continual rain and storms. Such weather was not welcome last Thursday when we had a whole day off; we went out just the same, and by three, had really moved the stones around in a muddy quarry located in a really soaking woods. Under these conditions, the return wasn't without a certain enchantment; with the sun out, it would have been more pleasant and rewarding. I went past the heronry, but evidently, there wasn't a bird in sight. Always speaking of the bad weather for awhile, it took the shape of sudden little showers which were heavy, but restricted, and which left part of the land bright, while the rest of the land, where the rain fell, was almost

172

like ink. The sight from our windows was quite novel; and especially one night when there was a full moon, there was also a beautiful, quasi-complete lunar rainbow whose colors were discernible without too much imagination on the part of observers; it's the first I've seen.

Victor wrote me again; he's been grappling with a puzzler, but seems to be carrying it off well, that's an indication of a good omen. I also received a letter from Uncle Cirice.[1]

I've just finished sending my plant fossils; right now they should be in Cambridge, but I haven't heard a word about them.[2] I'm ending my letter after a trip to the base of the cliffs; they didn't reveal anything important, but the weather was admirable. There was just a little mist to turn the sun red and to make the English Channel look like the Sea of Greenland.

Goodbye, dear Father and Mother; my love to you as well as Guiguite (thanks for her letter), Gabriel, Olivier and Joseph, the soldier.

For Mother: I now say Mass on the altar across from one where I said my first Mass; I don't forget you there.

Pierre

1. Cirice Teilard-Chambon, father of Marguerite and Alice. See *Letters from Paris,* letter 7.
2. See letter 66.

59

Dear Father and Mother,

It hardly seems possible that another two weeks have passed with almost no trace other than a couple of notches to mark the further completion of classes. It's the last of my scheduled classes quickly coming to an end; so that the time may be better filled, I'm preparing a public defense of my thesis for a young priest, and I can't complain. Then too, it will be the last time that I have such an honor. Meantime, I'm going to preach on Friday at the convent of the "Birds" at St. Leonard's. Otherwise, it doesn't give me much pleasure; I am trying to develop a style of public speaking, experience proving that those who wait too long to start end up unable to confront an audience. My audience won't be too intimidating at first; just the same, would Mother please keep this occasion in mind?

As I received news about Guiguite after a two-day delay, I was spared a lot of worry; I thought right away that the crisis must be over. But for you, who lived those moments one by one,

God allowed some difficult moments. I feel that you love all the more; but, I especially hope that Our Lord has kept track of all the anguish, particularly the anguish of these past few years, so that you will be rewarded later on. You'll find that those hours will have proven more fruitful than the years when we were most tranquil and happy.

I said my Mass for Guiguite the day after I learned of her new relapse.

Just to elaborate a bit on a point in my last letter, I'd like to tell Father that it wasn't a halo, but a real rainbow, that is to say, going out from the moon and seeming to touch the earth at its two extremities. At this time of the year, we often see halos around the sun.

Goodbye, dear Father and Mother; my love to you as well as Gabriel, Olivier and Joseph. I'm glad that Gonzague and M. Hains[1] get along well; he's a charming gentleman.

Pierre

1. Father Eugène Hains (1874–1963) was the spiritual director at the College of Mongré at that time; then he moved to Moulins (Bellevue). He became rector of several colleges in the Lyons Province.

60

Ore
December 20 [*1911*]

Dear Father,

    As I do every year, I'm writing to wish you a Merry Christmas, and at the same time, a Happy New Year; but this year I can do it more effectively: of my Christmas Masses, one will be for you, and you know how fervently I'll pray Our Lord to give you strength and consolation during this new year. Since my last Christmas wishes, one of us has gone to God, and you have had much to suffer. My poor Father, I've told you so often that the love which those remaining have for you is more intense, while the love of those who have gone is more powerful and undoubtedly closer. On the evening of the 24th, when you can hardly not remember all our other get-togethers, think that today's situation, albeit more austere and less sweet, is, in fact, more worthy of esteem. At that time, when you look at us, you can count on our paying you tribute; now, in a way you wouldn't have the courage to envision, the realization has begun. It seems that—scattered or suffering, or reduced in number as our family

176

is here on earth—it has never been as beautiful in God's eyes as it is today. Let us beseech Him so that the work He wills is accomplished, whatever it is; after all, the only real consolation is the knowledge that you have done your best to be faithful to the end.

Goodbye, my dear Father; once more, Merry Christmas. All my love to you.

Pierre

61

Dear Father and Mother,

When you receive this letter, Yéyé's departure will be very close; but it's fitting before all else, and despite the fact that it begins with a separation, to wish you and all those at Clermont a happy year for 1912. And really, can we say that it is starting badly? Olivier is taking his first slice of adult life bravely; that's good and it is normal. I'm confident that God will bless him—and you; He will reward the detachment which never caused you hesitation before making the sacrifice of one of your children. 1911 took Françoise from you, and 1912 separates you from one of your grown-up ones. Despite all appearances, and if we know how to see the hand of God in all things, we have to believe that these are good years all the same—and in certain respects, the best, because there was more to give. I will pray a lot for all of you on January 1st, and the Mass on the 4th will be for Yéyé. It's too bad that Boléo isn't in central Mexico any more. Through my friends here, I would have been able to arrange some contacts for

Olivier; California is still mission territory—served, I think, by Italian priests.

I don't have to ask, as I know you will keep me up on the news you receive about the trip—it will probably be a simple one taken in the comfortable coaches of some transcontinental.

On the 4th, I won't be able to look across the sea to Le Havre without deep feeling.

This letter is being written from Grove Ferry where I arrived Saturday evening after a defense of my thesis that was good, but not more striking than was necessary.[1] Since then, I've been more or less leading a hermit's life deep in Kent's countryside. Here in the county, there is nothing more picturesque than the downs toward Dover, and the great parks beside Ashford. The chalk has been levelled by erosion, and covered by a thick bed of alluvium and gravel; it makes nothing more than low hills interspersed with vast flooded grasslands. Where the valleys narrow and heighten, stand picturesque cottages which are often thatched and surrounded by huge young elms or, sometimes, green oaks. All the rest of the land is covered with immense, muddy fields which, ordinarily, are perfectly bare. Many are still planted with a certain kind of cabbage whose stalk is puffed out like a beet; little by little, these are eaten by the great flocks of sheep who leave the field trampled and unmentionably dirty as they go. Here and there are very large farms with immense thatched granges, yards filled with little donkeys moving around freely on the straw, and there's hay stacked all around.

A curious thing, while passing by such a place, I heard the whip crack, but I didn't see anyone ploughing, as I did in Hast-

1. This concerns the *Disputatio Theologica* on the Eucharist, which he discussed in his December 4th letter. See letter 33 as well.

ings. The land must be very pretty in the summer; now, it's a bit sad; I learned that the place is about to become an important mining center. Soundings made near Grove Ferry and all along the way from here to Dover, have revealed a lot of coal. It seems that the land is already being bought up. If drillings have begun when I'm about to go to Canterbury to make my Third Year, they will prove a precious geological resource.

Speaking of walks, yesterday, I went to the shore of the North Sea at Riculver. There's a little old village and an ancient church in ruin, whose two towers are outfitted with lights to guide the way to Tamise. Seen under a reddening sun, and through a mist which allows only a glimpse of the sea, the spot has its own penetrating poetry disturbed only by my getting slightly bogged in the marshes, thanks to a slippery plank . . .[2]

2. The rest of this letter is missing, but the following letters inform us.
During the year 1911, in the *Dictionnaire apologétique de la Foi catholique,* published under the direction of Father Adhémar d'Alès, in volume 2, there appeared an article called "Homme"; the fourth part: "L'homme devant les enseignements de l'Eglise et devant la philosophie spiritualiste," was signed by Father Teilhard de Chardin (cols. 501–514). Some passages are of interest. Column 505 on evolution reads: "We conclude that it is necessary to reject an evolution which, soldering man through all the fibers of his being, to all inferior forms of life or matter, only looks on him as the product of a transformation—be it from like to like, by reshuffling primitive composites—or be it more or less through a growth and development (due to a divine source) which would not bring an abrupt and deep rearrangement to an end, a wrenching free from the common run to place Humanity in a region of transcendence and stability."
In column 509, a classical dualism is still professed. (Perhaps it was in writing that page that Father Teilhard became aware of the weakness of that dualism.)
Column 512: "It is possible to grant many postulates in the evolutionary concept which has man coming into the world from an immanent generative force. Man did not dig a hole in nature when he came along, but through something in his very self, he was taken up into this vital determinism which governs the gradual appearance of different organisms on

PIERRE TEILHARD DE CHARDIN

the earth. He rose up at a time and under conditions dictated by the composite of physical and biological laws. He "grew" into the world rather than being grafted . . . But against the spirituality of the soul and our transcendence relative to other living things, what comes from that? Nothing."

Column 513: "As for the Christian view of man's dignity, it disappears when there is nothing but a quantitative and local anthropomorphic center . . ."

62

Dear Father and Mother,

I suppose that by the time this letter arrives, you will finally have received the first news from Boléo, and I pray that Olivier's horizon will continue to light up, the closer he comes to the Pacific. His account of the trip from New Orleans was very interesting; I'm convinced that California is a place to which a person gets attached quickly. Speaking of New Orleans, we have an American who comes from there; he tells us some very curious stories about the trouble some white people take to avoid the negroes; these poor negroes are obviously quite spurned, and to take an example, prevented from riding in the same car as whites; it seems that this ostracism isn't completely without reason. Only Catholicism is able to bring something out in these poor people; but in return, it has succeeded in establishing one or two negro congregations of nuns—something my American colleague considers a permanent miracle. I don't know if Olivier has had time to get some insight into the negro question.

In Hastings the weather continues to be mild, but quite nasty, with storms, rain and fog. The weather was good the day when the novices came; we took advantage and challenged them to a game of football on our field; as it turned out, they lost—more, even, than we would have liked. Definitively with Lent begins my last period of classes which will finish on March 22nd, —just in time for the ordination of new deacons. During Holy Week, I shall be practising my ministry a bit in France . . . near Boulogne, at Belle; that means in Yolande's very parish. I was invited, thanks to a Father from Champagne who was here last year to speak on the same occasion in the same place. The work isn't too foreboding: four or five sermons and some confessions; it's always an opportunity to do some good.

Goodbye, dear Father and Mother; my love and prayers to you and to all those at home.

Pierre

Can you send me Olivier's address?

63

Ore
March 22, 1912

Dear Father and Mother,

This is the last day of class. Tomorrow, I'll be given a list of quite varied questions on philosophy and theology. I'm expected to peg away at those with all my might for the next four months at the most. According to the majority who did this before, it's a very pleasant time—not only because you're in the house where classes are being held and you don't have to attend, —but more especially because of the enchantment which lies in being able to do some personal work, with all the books desirable, with the aim of synthesizing and clarifying all the ideas gathered from the past.[1] Experience will tell me what to make of it. In any case, the week in Belle can't be anything but a happy diversion; even though the audience is simple (with the exception of the deputy, if he pays me the honor of coming), I don't sense the fearlessness

1. The tradition of these months of independent study and preparation for final exams in theology is still followed in the scholasticates of the Society.

and confidence of an old veteran. I think I'll be leaving here on Tuesday of Holy Week to return on the following Tuesday. Boulogne isn't so far that I have to worry about the distress caused by the strike. Hastings, and more especially Ore Place continues to have very little idea about the nation's troubles. The only noticeable sign is that the trams from St. Helen have dwindled to one an hour. Besides, not being in touch with the outside, it's impossible to appreciate the situation.

The *Oceana* was wrecked just across from Hastings, a little west of the light-ship you saw in September (it's the only rotating light to be seen from Hastings) in the exact place where Tourville once beat the English. From Ore, you can see the masts, using field glasses, and you watch the movements of the tug boats; we were really aware of the tragedy. Bodies were washed up along the Hastings parade. For two days there has been a violent south wind with sudden showers, which makes it impossible or useless to salvage any of the ship's valuables.

Tomorrow and Sunday is the ordination of subdeacons and deacons. The 25th marks a year to the day since my own. The reform of the breviary and, up until now, the absence of an "ordo" following the new changes, makes it a bit harder to teach the young. On the 19th, I didn't forget that it has been 13 years since you let me leave; I didn't forget to pray especially that God bless you and reward you. Yesterday, Father's letter arrived; I'm very happy over the news about Olivier.

Goodbye, dear Father and Mother. My love to you. Tell Gabriel and Joseph that I didn't forget their birthdays on the 18th and 19th.

Pierre

64

Ore
April 10, 1912

Dear Father and Mother,

It's been an eternity since I last wrote. I had counted on sending you a letter from Belle; but there was no time. First of all, briefly, I was very happy with my stay there. Despite what you might imagine, there wasn't a mission (the curate recently gave one which lasted a whole week) but rather, it was to finish up Lent: a few sermons, confessions above all else, done in a way that the parishioners would be at ease with a stranger.

Once more, I've found that once a person knows what he wants to say, public speaking is an easy thing, even agreeable. Then too, Belle is a very amenable place for an apprenticeship.

My boat was late because of the many passengers; it also had to take ¾ of an hour to dock because of the low tide. I came ashore at Boulogne around nightfall, and happily, I found the pastor waiting for me on the dock.

If he hadn't been there, I would have gone to Rinxan (trusting in a directory) which is almost as far from Belle as Boulogne is;

with him and the car loaned by a parishioner (and not without having first gulped down a few generous slices of bread and butter, prelude to what awaited me during my whole stay), I arrived at the presbytery safe and sound around 9 p.m. My work for the week went something like this: Wednesday, building a repository and hearing women's confessions; Thursday, the Office, a visit to Yolande, and, in the evening, a sermon on the Passion. It's the day Yolande, accompanied by Charlotte, chose to come and hear me; since I was directed to "hold forth" for ¾ of an hour, it must have made her stew; but she was tactful enough not to mention it. Friday, it was the Office, some home visits, then a sermon. Saturday, Office and men's confessions. Easter Day, short sermons in the morning and a longer sermon in the evening.

In short, Belle is a good little parish; no villages to speak of, but only great farms spread out over rich pastures in the Wimereux valley, a shallow river which is rich in trout and other fish. At first glance, a French home is hardly distinguishable from one of its farms. Le Broc (I'm ignoring the spelling) embraces a large yard surrounded by stables; on each side of the house, there's a little garden, a bit like the vegetable garden at Sarcenat; the rest is a bit like the great prairies where the deputy's cows graze. The land is large and it isn't broken up. I found Charles in a corner near his fireplace; he had a two-week growth of beard and was laid up with a leg injured as he was trying to start up his car. Even though he claimed to be frayed (he has to be let loose) his humor wasn't changed over such a little matter. The rectory was more simple, but family-like and cordial, as everyone is over there. You will never know what a pleasure it was to hear these wonderful people speak, with their picturesque

187

expressions and their melodic speech. Even though it was Lent, between visits I must have had a number of "bistouilles" (coffee or some other drink with a drop of liqueur); I much would have preferred bread and butter when Church laws allowed. The cantor's family name is Scevola (the blacksmith jokingly said Scélérat) and the proper names ran: Poulet, Butor; —all of them were wonderful people.

When I left yesterday morning, Tuesday, it was rather hard on me. Charles asked one of my cousins, whose name I forget, and who proved to be extremely kind in taking me to Boulogne by car; a robust man appeared, wearing a long coat and large cap, and a fat moustache, the distinguished chauffeur type. He took me, with all his know-how and professional pride, over the winding roads of Wimereux, almost to Ambleteuse (where I once drank so much sea water with Albéric); finally, he let me off regally right at the boat for England. It was cold and clear; from Wimereux's hills you can see the cliffs of Dover as I vaguely remembered they looked from the windows at Haut-Buisson. An enchanting walk ended my trip to France. The return crossing was cold, but not too hard. I saw the landslide at the cliffs in Hastings; it happened halfway to Dover, and it's quite noticeable.

Now there's nothing more to do than resume preparation for the last exam; I assure you that in Belle, theology seemed really far away: it was the greatest rest. I'm finishing up rather quickly so that my letter can go off tonight. I keep praying for all of you and neither forgot you nor Guiguite last week. My love to you and the boys as well.

Pierre

P.S. Father asked me for H. Bremond's address. It is: 34 Place des Prêcheurs, Aix-en-Provence.[1]

---

1. Henri Bremond had been Pierre's professor (humanities class) at the college at Mongré.

65

Dear Father and Mother,

I've had two weeks to forget my stay in Belle, and now—without any fever—I'm right in the midst of preparing for final exams. Really and truly, this time has its charm, but I know it will come to an end. To make it more pleasant, we're having marvelous weather, almost too warm, which is beginning to pose a threat to the crops; the trees are turning green as far as the eye can see, but the grass isn't growing, and the fields are unbelievably dry. Like yourselves, we watched the eclipse with great interest; it covered 95% of the sun and made the sole mistake of coinciding with our dinner hour. Even though there isn't the total darkness enabling the halo to show, I still think that the most interesting things to watch are the lunar tints which the countryside takes on. It made Ore look beautiful.

Last Saturday, my geologist friend, Mr. Dawson,[1] came for a visit. He brought me some prehistoric remains (silex, elephant and hippopotamus, and especially, a very thick, well-preserved

1. See letter 43.

human skull) which he had found in the alluvium deposits not far from here; he did this in order to stir me up to some similar expeditions; but I hardly have time for that any more. He also brought two or three interesting things, and we sent some possibly rare leaf prints to Cambridge; only it takes a long time for them to answer.

I share Father's amazement over the courage and disinterested-ness of those American millionaires; as a whole, they were very brave on that poor *Titanic*[2] and that is comforting. I conclude that most of those people are worth more than they believed themselves to be, and that they really had occasion to show exactly what they were. The radio operators are making up a list of heroes.

Goodbye, dear Father and Mother. My love to you; I'm pray-ing for you and for good little Guiguite who must have really fretted over your delay in Clermont. May God's will be done.

Please thank Gabriel on my behalf, for his long letter from Nîmes and his card from Stes-Maries; I'll answer him soon. I hope Olivier will have sent you news; they always interest me so much. Decidedly, he's only missing some game.

Pierre

All the best to Joseph. I went past the heronry at Brede; the birds were on the branches and you could see them perfectly, since there weren't any leaves.

2. On its first crossing, the huge steamer struck an iceberg south of Newfoundland on the night of April 14th or 15th. There were more than 1500 victims. While the ship was sinking, the orchestra played the hymn, "Nearer, my God, to Thee."

66

Dear Father and Mother,

I was happy to learn through Father's note that Planchard was finally letting you go back to Sarcenat. Here, I will try my best to unite myself to you as you make the novena to Our Lady; I hope that Guiguite will be a bit better. The Blessed Virgin will choose the best thing; undoubtedly, we in the family will come to love God a bit more.

Here, my life continues to be very peaceful, and mixed with a good proportion of pleasant things. Once more, it's certainly going to be cut, as I will spend a couple of weeks near Brighton in a convent which doesn't have a chaplain; it's a change of scenery without keeping me from working; but since this isn't until the end of June, I'll write you about it in my next letter.

This week, the rain finally reached us; and it was about time. Not much rain fell, but the weather stayed humid, which makes up for it a little. All of a sudden, the countryside has become splendid; I saw many felled coppices in a place where, for hundreds of metres, the ground is completely violet with hyacinths; it's a fairyland. At least for a day, we've been treated to the clearest weather I've seen in four years. From atop Hastings cliffs, a person can not only distinguish Folkestone and Dover admirably, but also Gris-Nez and a long tip of France. An Englishman from here told us that on a similar occasion, Louis-Philippe—then on a visit to his father or his uncle (the Englishman's of course)—fell to his knees and rather snidely concluded that we Frenchmen must really love our country. Gris-Nez and the Boulognese shores, especially reminded me of Belle, whose poor curé must have had a bad week; his 50 electors found a means of putting 4 petitions together, and the kind mayor who received me so well is on the second ballot. Maybe you will be interested to know that Lord Ashburnham's daughter entered the convent of the Sacred Heart; had she married, she would have taken possession of Ashburnham when an aged uncle died; the estate would have gone to him when the present Lord died. Now the family is destined to die out and the land has no more chance to pass into the hands of Catholics. I really believe that the Ashburnhams couldn't have ended the line any better way; I wouldn't like to find myself a director of conscience called to make a decision in a similar case.

I received news from Cambridge; without disclosing any great new things, my plant collections constitute an "important contribution to botany," especially in making knowledge of several species more precise.[1] The ferns I found two weeks ago (they had large leaves with vast networks of veins) weren't known yet

1. See letter 58.

in the area in satisfying examples, at any rate. A study with photographic reproductions and drawings will be published. Goodbye, dear Father and Mother. My love and prayers.

Pierre

67

Bramber
June 3, 1912

Dear Father and Mother,

I'm writing to you from my new residence where I'm living an ideal little life of a hermit![1] Separated from the highly populated Brighton coast by the Downs, Bramber is right in the country, and the Towers is even more so. To top off this peace and poetry, I'm living all alone in a little isolated house with two rooms to myself and some swallows who nest in my windows. From that window I can see apple trees above everything else. There are also pigeons, chickens and a donkey, etc.: it's a complete picture of calm.

Here, I've found a sort of boarding school which is rather grandiose and is run by the "Ladies of the Blessed Sacrament"; there are a dozen or so religious, and around twenty children or young girls—some French, some English, or some other nationality; there are two little mulattoes who would delight Guiguite. Naturally, here as happened at Malvern, I'm still in the clutches

1. See letter 63.

of the extern Sister's solicitude; Mother shouldn't be at all worried over my welfare. The house shadowing the boarding school is an old, private, not too pretentious residence (a square flanked by four high cement towers with five or six deer heads decorating the portals, and what's better, all covered with vines); what I saw of the inside was very beautiful; the hallway and stairs are spacious, almost monumental; and especially as it is fitting to a convent, everything gleams with cleanliness.

It isn't hard to render my services: Mass at 7:15, Benediction at 6 in the evening—a few confessions, and unquestionably, 4 or 5 sermons; that's about all. This leaves me some leisure for theology and walks. I only went out once; that was yesterday; to see the whole situation, I climbed the hills closest to the house. You know what it's like, as you saw the "downs" from Folkestone: coasts which are two to three hundred metres high, admirably and softly rounded, covered with clipped grass; there's an occasional helmet of beech trees. This is broken now and then by a quarry which makes a glaring white spot. Bramber is located on a hill; the Adur, a little river, runs through there. From the crest of the closest hill I climbed, while reminiscing about peaks, I could follow the Downs as they stretched out to the west, turning north, and then returning, encircling the green and rolling region of Weald. In this huge, wooded basin, made lofty by a string of hills ending around Hastings, there were many things to see. Since there weren't any people around to show me, I tried my best to spot them with the aid of a map. I could spot the Cowfold Chartreuse (a branch of the Great Chartreuse; its present abbott is one of Mongré's former students) it seems; I really plan to walk there. I don't know if I'll do the same for the Praemonstratensian abbey at Storington. You must have seen the names in the newspapers three years ago when poor Tyrrell died, —you know, the man who died at the home of the all-too-well-known Miss Peter, near here.[2]

With all of that, I haven't told you about the day I spent in Lewes (near New-Haven) at my friend Mr. Dawson's[3] home; it was on my way here. For that day, we planned an excursion to the famous alluvial deposits at Uckfield (north of Lewes); the prehistoric remains I mentioned in one of my letters over a month ago came from there. I began with a hearty English breakfast in Mr. Dawson's very tidy home: it's a very comfortable dwelling nesting right in the middle of the ruins of the old castle which overlooks Lewes.

Mrs. Dawson is an Irish woman born in Bordeaux. One son is in the colonial army in the Sudan, and is cluttering the house with antelope heads.

I was received cordially. Around 10 o'clock, we were in Uckfield where Professor Woodward joined us. He is director of the British Museum's paleontology division,[4] and is a little man with salt-and-pepper hair, plus a rather cold appearance. At three o'clock, armed with all the makings for a picnic, we started off in the car. After going across Uckfield Castle's grounds, we were left off on the hunting ground: a grassy strip 4-5 metres wide, which skirts a wooded path leading to a farm. Under this grass, there's a 50 centimeter layer of gravel which is gradually being

2. On the death of Tyrrell, and the circumstances that surround it, you will find some help with the bibliography in Blondel and Valensin, *Correspondance*, vol. 2 (1957), pp. 70–84. That same year, Miss Mand Peter (d. 1942) published 2 volumes in London, *Autobiography and Life of George Tyrrell*.

3. See letter 65. For the first meeting with Dawson, see letter 14.

4. See *Letters from Paris*, letters 29, 32. Also, letter 70 below.

removed to be used for roads. A man was there to help us dig; armed with picks and sifters, we worked for several hours and finally had success. Dawson discovered a new fragment of the famous human skull; he already has three pieces of it, and I myself put a hand on a fragment of an elephant's molar; this find made me really worth something in Woodward's eyes. He jumped on the piece with the enthusiasm of a youth and all the fire that his apparent coldness covered came out. To meet my train, I had to leave before the other two were to abandon their search.

The first elephant tooth gave me the same feeling hunters have when they catch their first goose.

I still don't know exactly how long I shall be here; probably until the 17th; but that would positively be the last day. Yesterday, I received Mother's letter and Guiguite's safe and sound.

I must close for now, dear Father and Mother. On the 7th, my Mass will be for Françoise and all of you.

Pierre

68

Dear Father and Mother,

Tomorrow evening, I'm leaving the Towers; and as I shall arrive in Hastings just in time to make a triduum for vows (until the 21st) it's urgent that I send you a letter before leaving here.

First, all your news arrived quite regularly, up until Joseph's last letter (I thank him so much for that, and promise to answer him). To my satisfaction, I learned that Olivier is settled, but what must the mother of this dare-devil think! He's certainly in a hard school, but it's really what he needs. I shall not forget to keep him in my daily Masses.

My stay here continued as it began, in the greatest tranquillity, and with a certain regularity: work in the morning, walk in the evening. I felt rejuvenated at my table listening to the little children telling their tales in the garden while, at the same time, there floated in echoes of the same piano pieces Guiguite used to practise when I worked with Croze.

Now I know the Bramber area well, and have found it more beautiful every day. First, it has been ages since I've had the big free spaces in front of me that the Downs offered. With the gentians and the altitude at least, many points reminded me of Rocquet's plateaux. The grass is very clipped; only certain sides are covered with Juniper trees; all of it smells dry and good. You see sheep in abundance ("South-Downs," naturally), and near the great Steyning park, I even saw a pasture with little shaggy Scottish long-horned cattle—like the ones we saw at Ashburnham, I think.

As far as wildlife is concerned, there are peewits building their nests, wood pigeons in the bushes, and half-tame hares. Weald's plains and rolling land are very pleasant, fewer coppice trees and more sunken roads; the greenery seemed more rich than at Hastings. On the way to Parkminster, which I'll discuss later, it was hard to believe that the route crossed Vialles meadows for two or three miles; only the oaks were less lovely. I must mention that the area is almost a continual string of parks.

Parkminster is the only Carthusian monastery left (under Henry VIII there were 10!). It is under the patronage of St. Hugues of Lincoln;[1] its bursar is P. de Falconnet, formerly from Mongré. (Maybe I have already told you.) I went there last Monday and couldn't have been received more fraternally. The buildings are huge; thirty years ago, they were solidly constructed of lovely gray stone, and planted on 800 hectares of grounds which are almost all meadows or woods.

1. Hugues d'Avalon (Dauphin) bursar of the "Grand Carthusian Monastery," became the third prior of Witham, one of the two Carthusian monasteries founded by Henry II to expiate the murder of St. Thomas Becket; Bishop of Lincoln in 1186, he died in 1200.

I saw the Chartreuse from top to bottom, drank the traditional little glass—and returned very struck by the powerful affirmation of the supernatural the life of these men represents. They neither work like the Trappists, nor produce books as do the Benedictines. Truly, those people who only want to see human progress in the world could truthfully say that the life of the Carthusian is good for nothing; and it is good that it can be said this way by some men in the Church; you can't be misunderstood.

To answer one of Father's less flattering remarks about the Towers, I would tell him that the stag heads are very authentic. Moreover, I found out that the house (and even the old family homestead) is presently owned by a great English lady who lives and dresses under the name of Sister Marie-Agnes. She's a convert who was dissuaded from making her vows in 1900 so that she could better support the Congregation. She's quite intelligent and rather unique; she has read many things and it is extremely interesting to talk to her. You can find her in a large sitting room in the company of a large cat which sleeps in an upholstered basket; she herself is seated in a large armchair. I think that the abbesses from the old days must have been exactly like that. For this one, at least, a certain apparent comfort doesn't detract from her being a very holy soul.

Yesterday, she lent me Benson's *The Light Invisible* which I hadn't read yet; but there wasn't enough time for me to do a proper reading. *In the Convent Chapel* pleased me very much; but it must have lost a lot in translation.[2]

2. In imitation of this work by Benson, he was to write at Nant-le-Grand near Verdun, in October, 1916, *Le Christ dans la Matière, trois histoires comme Benson*. See *Ecrits du temps de la guerre* (1965), p. 88. See letter 54 above.

This evening, I went for a goodbye walk to the Downs; there was a violent downpour, but I was rewarded by a view of fresh and unbelievable tints. I brought back an orchid bud and some rose orchids which I'd like Ore's botanists to analyze.

Goodbye, dear Father and Mother; my love to you as well as to Gabriel, Guiguite and Joseph. I pray for you.

Pierre

69

Dear Father and Mother,

This is probably the next to the last time I'll be writing to you from Ore; this will probably be the last if I keep up the present pace of correspondence. My exam is set for July 14th, and after this date, I'll have no reason for staying here. As for my final lot, be it at the beginning of August or after the feast of the Assumption,[1] I still know absolutely nothing. But I imagine that before the end of this week, I will know a bit of what to expect. I'll tell you what I can.

Meantime, the days are passing rather tranquilly, and I'm developing a noticeable detachment toward the things which habitually make up the life of this scholasticate. As I go through the last of these, I see my year being unstrung—one of the bad sides of the end of this period—I don't hide the fact that the Orcine retreat captivated me; it's one of the last fields of evange-

1. It is usually August 15th, every year, that the new assignments are published for the following year.

lization I would have chosen; but I do know that this poor mother didn't put any malice into it, and wishes above all for the good of her loved ones.

I like to hope that heaven will reward her for her confidence by granting me to be good for something, even in my own country.

Successively, this week, I went to say Mass at the church in old Hastings, and then at the Reparatrix convent. I hadn't seen these two places since August. Both reminded me of the good times we spent there together.

When I came back from Bramber, I found Olivier's letter here, dated May 25th. It didn't say anything you don't already know except, perhaps, that the short letter he sent after the fire was written post-haste. He had slept for 16 consecutive hours. It followed a night busy with making the Mexicans "pivot" in honor of the god, Michot. There was a line about lucerne and another on frigates.

Goodbye, dear Father and Mother; my love and prayers for you, not to mention Guiguite, Gabriel, Joseph and Gonzague.

Pierre

70

Dear Father and Mother,

This morning, I received the bad news of Gonzague's failure. Surely Our Lord isn't spoiling you with consolations here on earth. All of that would be amply compensated if Gonzague were to be decisive about a career suited to his taste and for which he would have the courage to really work. I assure you that I have great confidence in the choice of events which God sends, be they eminently disagreeable, and you shouldn't be upset about it. You'll see; everything will turn out well.[1]

Tomorrow is my exam.[2] Here's a glimpse of what is to follow: Tuesday I leave for Paris where I am to stay until Saturday evening (M. Cisternes, 5 rue du Regard). From there, I'm going

1. This is the expression of spiritual principles to which he will always remain faithful.
2. Father Teilhard successfully passed his final exam in theology and this was equivalent to the Doctorate in Theology.

to Lyons and then to la Barollière[3] (Gonzague knows it) where I stay until the evening of Sunday, the 21st. There, I'll make my own retreat which will finish for the feast of St. Ignatius; around August 5th, I'll be coming to see you; to confirm that last date, I'm waiting for a reply from the curate in Orcines. Naturally, I'll write to you in the meantime. After that, the use of my time hasn't been absolutely fixed; the East doesn't seem to be on my list for the coming year.

For the time being, caught between an impending exam and the chaos of moving, it's hard to believe that I'll be leaving Ore Place in three days.

Last Wednesday, Dr. Woodward of the British Museum paid me a visit; he has "plundered" my collection enough to make me feel flattered. I now have free access to South Kensington, if I ever need it.

Goodbye, dear Father and Mother; my love and prayers to all of you. It will be so good to see you 2 weeks from now. Mother would be very wrong were she to make too much fuss over my natural taste for the audience at Orcines.

I had written without too much insight into what it was all about.

Pierre

La Barollière's address is "N. D. de Barollière, par St Paul en Jarrez, Loire."

3. Spiritual retreat house, above Saint-Chamond on the side of Mt. Pilat. Gonzague had just made a retreat there, a custom usually followed by students of the Jesuits. See *Etablissements, op. cit.,* vol. I, art. "Brollière."